Modern Landscape

Michael Spens

Modern Landscape

To Janet

Introduction

Landscape Architecture Today

As the twenty-first century proceeds there is evidence of a growing interest in landscape as a field of study and professional activity. This interest is widespread, and ranges well beyond the immediate professions of architecture, landscape architecture and town and regional planning. The landscape issue has become one of society's central preoccupations, a situation to which a number of factors have contributed. There is, for example, the dramatic increase in pressure for building development and its related infrastructure, in both urban and rural locations. There is also a growing concern over sustainability and maintenance of healthy eco-systems, especially in the northern hemisphere. Linked to these concerns is an awareness of the failure by politicians at all levels to take steps that would remedy the situation. There is also a realization among professionals, academics and other informed bodies that the breadth of interest in the topic and the urgency of the issues involved has engendered little new discussion on the subject. They are aware, too, that we have achieved little new understanding of the cultural significance of landscape today, despite the fact that landscapes and gardens have traditionally acted as vehicles for new ideas ever since the Renaissance.

Utopia, a holistic concept, was still cherished for much of the twentieth century. In the twenty-first century we have deliberately foregone the Utopian ideal, allowing the idea itself to become obsolete. It is to Arcadia, a far more fragmented concept, that we look in this new century for the possibility of fulfilment. This ideal encompasses the establishment of individual areas of natural sanctuary that are somehow immune from violence and devastation. Landscape has always offered us such psychological respite.

At the close of the twentieth century, it was argued that the design of the landscape was of greater consequence than architecture *per se*. It was proposed that we should give at least equal priority to the 'greening' of the planet, as to the architecture which had proliferated across it. The idea of 'place-form' which, to use Max Bill's definition, runs in direct contrast to 'product-form', has become acceptable, and yet until very recently discourse has been limited in range and scope.[1]

A small group of conferences/symposia were held towards the end of the last century in an attempt to remedy the lack of a debate about landscape. An important precursor had been the symposium held in October 1988 at the Museum of Modern Art, New York, entitled *Landscape and Architecture in the Twentieth Century*. Contributions by Kenneth Frampton, John Dixon Hunt, Geoffrey Jellicoe and Vincent Scully were published in a book edited by the directing curator, Stuart Wrede, with several others under the title *Denatured Visions* in 1991. The overwhelming portion of the papers was retrospective and historical, a factor which however helped to raise the level of discussion and focus on existing socio-cultural dilemmas.[2]

The Villa Medici and its garden in Fiesole was a fifteenth-century utopia, a humanist, neoplatonic Ideal

Villa Madama (c.1516). Original design by Raphael, followed by Giulio Romano with gardens designed by Francesco da Sangallo. The building embraced nature, with long views to the Appenines and Rome

New Meanings, New Issues and Redefinitions

The activities of Land Artists and Installation Artists since the early 1970s have acted as a catalyst upon the work of landscape designers. There is an established body of practising landscape architects, all of them deeply committed and yet largely traditional in their approach to planting and design. There is also a small but growing number of recently-recognized designers who have sought to reconcile in their work the demands of sustainability, resource planning and aesthetics, to create a new precedent for the twenty-first century. Their work adds momentum to changes in perception, and also provides a valid extension to the landscape tradition that has evolved over the last few centuries. However, these designers all operate firmly within a Modernist framework.

To define the Modern Landscape in the twenty-first century we must recognize the longstanding, slow trajectory of development in landscape and garden design over the previous century. Modernism is a timeless category. The idea of the modern gathered pace as early as the eighteenth century in Europe. The diaspora of new thinking generated by the European Enlightenment was driven by new discoveries in science and by the dramatic revisions in philosophical thought spearheaded by David Hume, Edmund Burke and Immanuel Kant in particular.

The conventional Modernist view of the past was essentially one in which the critical eighteenth-century transformation in European thought seemed already to constitute a background to modern discourse. This background also encompassed the latter part of the Renaissance, and with it the familiar language of classicism. It is equally important to recognize that the classical cultures of the Hellenistic and Roman epochs were generic influences too. Instrumental here were the early writings of Plato, Socrates and indeed Heraclitus.[3]

In 1785 James Hall produced his seminal essay on *The History and Principles of Gothic Architecture*, in which he succeeded in overturning Vasari's old premise that the Gothic was 'monstrous and barbarous, being void of all order and rather deserving the name of disorder and confusion'.[4] Then, in 1794, Dupuis published his apparently sacrilegious text, *The Origin of All Faiths: or the Universal Religion.*[5] Fissures were appearing in the structure of classical learning. The possibility that divinity was to be recognized purely as the essence of nature threw open the floodgates. The Enlightenment beliefs about a clockwork, 'mechanical' universe were becoming less confident, even within their own century.

It is important to recognize that such early turbulence over the classical landscape of eighteenth-century European thought could not have been seriously addressed without the dramatic advances made in the mechanical and life sciences. Exploratory voyages in the Southern Hemisphere and biological and horticultural discoveries had assisted this shift in perception. The reappraisal of landscape within the transformation of critical reason, which spread from Edinburgh to London, and from St Petersburg and Paris

Claude Lorrain, (1600–82) *Pastoral Caprice with the Arch of Constantine*, Collection Duke of Westminster. Lorrain was one of the greatest masters of idealized landscape painting. He was fascinated by the 'Golden Age' of classical antiquity. In the countryside around Rome, the Roman *campagna*, he drew inspiration from a wealth of classical ruins

The Fountain of the Nymph at the Château Marly-le-Roi, Yvelines, France (1713), Archives Nationale, Paris. 'Garden Architecture – Arcadia Transposed'). Another example of classical inspiration

to Geneva, Naples and Palermo, hinged upon the new fields of botany and plant husbandry. Botanical Gardens, like museums of natural history, were beginning to be established in the main centres of learning.

The spread of science-based learning seems now to have been in direct conflict with entrenched opposition to the growth of knowledge about natural phenomena. The idea of an idealized landscape, rooted in the manifold conventions of the early Renaissance, predated such progress. Similarly, the conventions of landscape design drew their provenance from earlier European roots.

Such concepts stemmed from the walled garden on the one hand, and the idea of 'wilderness' on the other. As a concept, the walled garden had developed from the Persian paradise garden, and was seen as a sanctuary from the wild forest of mystery and danger. Today, it is of course the latter that offers sanctuary in ecological terms. The roots of such a definition are ancient. As far back as Giovanni Bocaccio's *Decameron* (1358) the green garden of Paradise is celebrated. For Bocaccio's contemporary Francesco Petrarch (1304–74), the *veduta*, or 'view', associated with the Renaissance was already a powerful indicator in literature; the view he describes while skirting the Alps already has the ring of the eighteenth-century Grand Tour:

> 'To our rear are the Alps, separating us from Germany with their snowclad peaks rising into the clouds, into heaven; before us stand the Apennines and innumerable cities. The Po itself lies at our feet, separating the flat fields in a giant curve.'[6]

And yet, it seems that only shepherds, hermits and satyrs inhabited the stylized Renaissance landscapes outside the walls.

By the time of the eighteenth-century English landscape painter Richard Wilson, landscaped parks represented 'the happy rural idyll', regardless of rural poverty.[7] Such was the culture experienced in 1786 by Thomas Jefferson, future President of the newly-established United States. Back to his Monticello in Virginia went a copy of Thomas Whately's *Observations on Modern Gardening*.[8] Although not a follower of the plant propagator Linnaeus, Jefferson practised a humanized version of horticulture, notably diaristic, assisted by the Linnaean scientific method of plant identification.

It is at this juncture that the true precedent for Modernism in landscape design can be seen emerging in the combination of a natural, pastoral aesthetic with a scientific basis. This combination has been cyclical in landscape history. The European tradition of skilful land and plant husbandry could of course be traced back to Virgil.[9] The iconography of landscape itself, however, was to be dramatically renewed through science. Viewed against such precedent, landscape as 'backdrop' is particularly significant, crystallizing in the paintings of Claude Lorrain (1600–82) and Gaspar Poussin (1613–75). Their environments are composed of buildings fused with geologically explicit terrain. There remain the stylized figures and hermits in the rocks within the essentially tamed landscapes of the Roman *campagna*.

If the idea of the 'Picturesque' landscape was purveyed successfully in

Kimberley Hall, Norfolk (1763). Park by Lancelot 'Capability' Brown. Here the natural landscape was recreated as Arcadia, a 'happy rural idyll'

Benjamin Zobel, *A Hermit and His Dog* (c1800), a picture painted in layers of coloured sand on a canvas support by King George IV's confectioner

Lake Pyramid in Branitz Park (1846–71) one of three pyramids designed by Furst Hermann von Puckler-Muskau

this way, it was not that vision, but rather that of the 'sublime', that Jefferson took with him to America. The landscapes of Lancelot 'Capability' Brown endorsed a familiarity with a nature which was scientifically explicit, but aspired also to the inexplicable 'Sublime' which Jefferson's contemporaries were to record as they explored their own continent. Jefferson had visited key Brownian schemes in England in 1786, and was himself familiar with the work of botanists such as Charles Alston (d.1760) and John Hope (d.1786), who intermingled in their research freely with mineralogists and natural scientists. The lake and park at Kimberley, Norfolk (1763), was a typical example of a 'Brownian' encounter with the 'wild' under controlled conditions.[10] Only in the United States of America did the full meaning of the wild reaches of the continent, newly explored under Jefferson, enhance the European concept of the Sublime.

Post-Enlightenment, Modernism and the Inherited Culture of Landscape and Garden Design

'Architecture is not art, it is a natural function. It grows out of the ground like animals and plants.'
Fernand Léger

The manner in which Enlightenment concepts survived industrialization, and remained models throughout the nineteenth and twentieth centuries, is one which seems for the most part to have supported rather than inhibited conventional Modernist philosophy. However, these concepts acted as models for modern landscape design, and came to represent an intellectually self-perpetuating cultural paradigm for twentieth-century landscape designers. It is the effect of this model, and its influence on the scope and potential development of contemporary landscape design, that makes it necessary to develop new thinking, and to make major realignments to the parameters of twenty-first century design.

Landscape architecture evolved its own form of modernity a generation later than architecture, in response to a different set of priorities. High social purpose did not predominate here, although social planning did play its part. Stylistic considerations were less imperative, less dominated by the functional creed that drove International Modernism in architecture.

An examination of the theoretical basis for a contemporary landscape tradition often reveals a clear divergence between the development of modern architecture and landscape. Modernist influence on the stylistic aspect of early garden design was often derived from Cubism, but this was not broadly-based enough to form any template for expansion. European landscape design produced no coherent equivalent to the avant-garde in architecture. Individual contributions remained isolated and fragmented. The Bauhaus significantly, and also tragically, offered no course in garden or landscape design. In its midst was the painter Paul Klee, whose imagined landscapes were to inspire landscape designers elsewhere. The painter

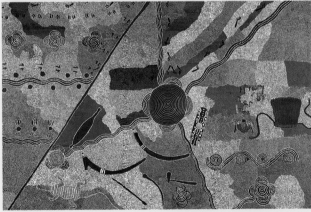

The socialist dream encapsulated by David Wild's Collage, *Constructed Socialism*, c.1930, from *Fragments of Utopia*, 1998

Tim Leura Tjapaltjarri, Anmatyerre (c 1939–84), *Rock Wallaby Dreaming* (1982), synthetic polymer paint on canvas, 120.8 x 179 cm (Purchased from Admission Funds, 1987, National Gallery of Victoria, Melbourne). Ancient Aboriginal mapping of tribal territories and their contained sacred mythologies

9

Johannes Itten taught at the Bauhaus from 1919–23, a key formative period, and later was supportive of modern garden projects in Zurich. He was followed, but only in Zurich, by Max Bill (1927) whose subsequent interest in the subject was also valuable. Tragically for European landscape design, however, the Bauhaus missed a critical opportunity in the 1920s, when landscape and garden design could have grown in unison with other aspects of contemporary art and design. It was left primarily to America to develop such a culture, and it grew well there.

Precepts in Transition

There was, nonetheless, a major transformation taking place in Europe at the time. Motivated by the search for social progress, the effects were felt chiefly in the fields of regional and urban planning. Such developments were to be instrumental in the re-ordering of conventional priorities. They also served to challenge the nineteenth-century assumption, engendered by industrial institutions, that natural resources were inexhaustible and that all development was a form of natural growth that could spread unchecked. Two great natural scientists, Sir Patrick Geddes (1854–1932) and Professor Sir D'Arcy Thompson (1860–1948) were instrumental in bringing a solidly-based intellectual discourse to environmental science. The former legitimized the scientific basis for planning human settlements, and the latter demonstrated underlying principles of organic and plant growth. Their contemporary, Sir Ebenezer Howard (1859–1928) had already pioneered the ideal garden city plan with his prototype Welwyn Garden City. The German architect-planner Ernst May was soon able to take this further in his Hellerhof Siedlung near Frankfurt (1929–32). May offered housing that respected the site's topology, and was successfully integrated with the form and contour of the landscape. In the 1970s Manfred Tafuri had commented that such layouts offered only an anti-urban Utopia. In retrospect, however, we know that Arcadia was already beckoning. In Russia, a focus at this time on habitat-planning for leisure, albeit short-lived, also revealed similar aspirations.[11]

Despite these innovations, there was no European equivalent to Frederick Law Olmsted (1822–1903). In America, Olmsted had laid out the theoretical basis for landscape design at a truly professional level. Although strong in the defence of formality, he adopted a naturalistic approach in his own designs for important city parks, inspired by a belief in the social imperative of providing city-dwellers with environments where nature prevailed. Soon afterwards, the architect Frank Lloyd Wright displayed a sensitivity to landscape unheard of among other architects at the time. The Kaufmann House, Fallingwater (1934–7), famously colludes with an existing waterfall: building and site are indivisible.

Other American practitioners, such as Jens Jensen (1860–1951) with Columbia Park in Chicago, or Fletcher Steele (1885–1971) in California, extended the realm of landscape design. However slight the effect of their

Gabriel Guevrékian's Cubist garden, designed to complement the Modernist design of the Villa Noailles, Hyères, France (1925)

Le Corbusier, 'La Mer Près A Mutril', 13/8/31 (Sketchbooks Vol 1, p.427). Le Corbusier romanticized landscape in his sketches and urban concepts

Adalberto Libera, Casa Malaparte, Capri, Italy (1935). An early example of the Modernist recognition of building within landscape features

work at first, it eventually prompted a nationwide movement. In the meantime, Garret Eckbo, Dan Kiley and James Rose were installed at Harvard in the late 1930s. The Canadian-British designer Christopher Tunnard also landed on his feet there, following disappointments in England.

European garden design itself encompassed a paucity of Modernist projects. The gardens by Gabriel Guevrekian and Robert Mallet-Stevens in France in the 1920s drew inspiration from Cubist painting, but this was primarily stylistic. While the avant-garde of modern architects dominated theoretical discussion, and built experimentally, little recognition was given to landscape or garden art. Ernst Cramer made his debut with a pool garden at the Zurich Cantonal Horticultural Show (ZUGA, 1933). Gustav Ammann also exhibited at ZUGA, displaying his Colour Garden, with its unusual organic form and innovative combination of plants. Viewing the work of Cramer and Ammann, the international critic Camillo Schneider was prompted to comment, 'the garden of the future will have to be very different in character, doing full justice to the plants, as well as developing artistic quality from the nature of the biological organism.'[12] The 1925 Paris Exposition of Modern Decorative and Industrial Arts and the 1933 Zurich Show mark the period in which Modernism at last engaged definitively with landscape, albeit only in small-scale gardens. These were isolated moments, though. Generally, the 'over-gardened English Garden', lamented in that context by Peter Latz as late as 1998, still prevailed.[13]

Architects, too, were aware of the change that was taking place. In the 1920s Le Corbusier had paid homage to landscape at Mutril. Alvar Aalto commented on vernacular building formations wholly integrated with their Italian landscapes. Hans Scharoun recognized site contour and place. Bruno Taut's Alpine Architecture (1919), a mountain fold for human habitat, integrated this with nearby industrial zoning without spoiling the integrity of the mountain itself. By the mid-1930s a real shift was becoming apparent. In the visitors' centre at Cheddar Gorge in Somerset, England (1934), Geoffrey Jellicoe worked with Russell Page to set his Modernist scheme harmoniously within a rock-riven gorge. Adalberto Libera fitted the structure of his Casa Malaparte island house off Capri (1935) deep within the immediate 'place-form', and Le Corbusier's house at La Lelle-St Cloud (Villa Felix, 1935), near Paris, in a radical departure from previous orchestrations, was partially interred within its site.

These significant and timely revisions of building with place-form were little heeded by critics until the postwar revision of the modern. Then, theory was again enriched, not so much by conventional aesthetic discourse as by engagement with scientific discovery. This revision of priorities was not, however, widespread. In the early part of the century garden designers had continued resolutely to ignore these new developments, and they flourished well into the 1930s along familiar lines. Harold Peto in England continued to design grandly for wealthy patrons. In Italy, but mainly for English clients, Cecil Pinsent followed suit. Both were essentially skilful classicists. In the

Geoffrey Jellicoe worked experimentally to design the Visitors' Centre, Cheddar Gorge, Somerset, England (1934)

A Summary Map, showing water and land features of Philadelphia Metropolitan area, designed by Ian McHarg, who spearheaded the ecological commitment to landscape architecture

1930s the Brazilian Roberto Burle Marx designed landscapes that reflected the influence of European Cubist painters. His work gained an early following in the United States, thus introducing the force of modern art to the landscape.

Before the Second World War broke out, there were already intimations of an international movement of contemporary landscape design. By 1950, Garret Eckbo and Dan Kiley were already working within their own modern idiom. In 1953, when the architect and landscape designer Peter Shepheard published his *Modern Gardens*, Ian McHarg was developing his rare combination of landscape design, ecology and town planning at the University of Pennsylvania. His seminal publication *Design with Nature* (1969) made a considerable impact, reviving the ecological commitment to landscape architecture that was to be a key to its future role. Shepheard himself moved to the University of Pennsylvania, aware that landscape design was undergoing a transformation at last.

It is hard to avoid the conclusion that the gestation of the modern landscape from the 1930s onwards occurred almost entirely in the United States. Its development was the responsibility of a relatively small group of practitioners centred in California, at Harvard, and in Pennsylvania. The academic recognition of their work was one of its chief strengths.

Geoffrey Jellicoe had himself directed the Architectural Association School in London during the Second World War. In 1943 he designed and initiated a 50-year programme of landscaped spoil reclamation in the Peak District National Park, Derbyshire (Blue Circle Co, 1943–95), inspired by the American Abstract Expressionist painter Jackson Pollock. Jellicoe was to lead English landscape design away from the small-garden perspective. In practice he developed landscapes that still engaged with history and precedent, but also reflected the development of scientific thought. His work was greatly influenced by the American philosopher John Dewey (1859–1952).

The Decades of Recovery
In 1938 Christopher Tunnard set the pace for an engagement with Modernism in his seminal work *Gardens in the Modern Landscape*, a book that attracted attention in both Britain and America. Subsequently, the Californian Garret Eckbo laid down a Modernist creed in his publication *Landscape for Living* (1950). In it he set out the first clear and unequivocal explanation of modern landscape architecture to be published since Tunnard's book of 1938. Eckbo set out six key requirements for the designer:

1: Denial of historical styles
2: Concern for space and pattern
3: A social agenda
4: Abandonment of the axis
5: Plants can act as 'sculpture'
6: Full and close integration in domestic cases of garden and house.

Roberto Burle Marx, Garden of the Hospital da Lagao, Rio de Janeiro (1957)

Gustav Piechl, Austrian Television Station, Aflenz (1976–9). The intention to integrate the architectural form within the landscape

By 1953 McHarg and Shepheard were at University of Pennsylvania and Tunnard was at Harvard. Such was the build-up in the United States of imported talent, mostly from Europe, covering both landscape theory and its practice in an expanding context. To this list must also be added Luis Barragán whose brilliant experimentation at El Pedregal, Mexico (1945–50) prefigured his Las Arboledas (1958–62) outside Mexico City.

Until the 1970s there was little exchange between America and Europe in the field of landscape design, and even less mutual awareness. Instead, it was exposure to the Abstract Expressionist art of Barnett Newman, Jackson Pollock and Milton Avery that stimulated and inspired European landscape designers. The subsequent development in America of Land Art was to become the most dramatic source of ideas.

By the 1980s, a discussion led by the Japanese American sculptor Isamo Noguchi was considerably enriched by the implied return to primary structure explicit in the work of such American artists as Robert Morris, Don Judd and Carl André. There was no comparable British source of inspiration.

In Europe, architects had initiated a line of development that was not unrelated. Research by South African architect Rex Martienssen into Greek Temple paths and routes (1956) had in the early 1960s been disseminated to add new force to the idea of space and the material reality of the route.[14]

Perhaps of greater relevance here is the path pursued by the American Land Artists Robert Smithson, Richard Serra, Robert Irwin and, from the late 1970s, Richard Long, Andy Goldsworthy and Ian Hamilton Finlay in Britain. Geoffrey Jellicoe's Kennedy Memorial Garden, Runnymede, England (1964) was followed by Ian Hamilton Finlay's Stoneypath in successfully incorporating its own allegorical content. But as a precursor to the genre, Ernst Cramer's apparently Minimalist Poet's Garden, Zurich (1959) is equally relevant here.

From the mid-1960s there also existed a strand of art which bore close affinities to emergent landscape thinking. The Italian Arte Povera movement added zest to the landscape debate, and both Sol le Witt and Jan Dibbets contributed. In due course, the closely detailed, poetic landscapes and routes of Georges Descombes came to bear out this tendency towards Minimalism in art and landscape design.

Post-Industrial Environmental Design and Land Art
The revision of priorities in the closing quarter of the twentieth century was to lead, as we have seen, to a renewed awareness of landscape as a finite resource. The demand for sustainability began to be applied to new landscapes, just as it was to new architecture. The designers of these landscapes were mindful of the fragility of the environment, sensitive to policies of conservation, and opposed to the exploitation of the past.

At last, a new template was emerging, whereby architects, engineers and landscape designers worked to a common scientific and cultural agenda. At first, this apparently Post-modern engagement occured within a plethora of

Geoffrey Jellicoe, Earle's Cement Works, Peak District National Park, Derbyshire, (1979). Projection of spoil transformation scheme

In Poets' Garden, Zurich, (1959), Ernst Cramer explored a Minimalist dimension in garden landscape design

Robert Irwin, Getty Center Garden, Los Angeles, (2001)

seemingly disconnected ideas and concepts. However, in the later 1980s it become creatively recharged, as we have seen, by Land Art, Installation Art, and Arte Povera, with its influence on the growth of Minimalism.

> But how can Man withdraw himself from the fields
> Where will he go, since the earth is one huge unbounded field?
> Quite simple – he will mark off a portion of the field by means of walls
> Which set up an enclosed finite space over against amorphous,
> limited space.
> Jose Ortega y Gasset

Robert Smithson's famous *Spiral Jetty* (1970) could have been inspired by this poem. Smithson and his friend the sculptor Richard Serra were acutely concerned that their work was becoming ensconced within a continuation of the Picturesque tradition. They worked to negate such thinking, and to offer landscape designers an inspirational path to 'the Sublime' in the landscape.[15]

Definitions of the Sublime have preoccupied contemporary critics: the architectural historian Colin Rowe qualified 'beauty' as a quality 'to be found somewhere in the terrain between the 'Picturesque' and the 'Sublime'.[16] Where indeed was Smithson's *Spiral Jetty* lodged? Smithson claimed that the Picturesque was 'like a sublime tree struck by lightning in a Picturesque English garden of the eighteenth century'.[17] It was precisely such considerations, grappled with by artists in the early 1970s, that landscape designers had spurned. Soon afterwards, however, landscape architecture revealed a clear shift of paradigm from primarily aesthetic considerations to those showing an ecological priority. When compared to architecture itself, the significance of this transition was that it allowed time for landscape architects to come fully to terms with innovations in the broader realm of art and culture. However, it must be admitted that in the past two decades most have experienced difficulties in bringing art to bear effectively upon the environment. To integrate creative initiatives from landscape art within their work has required a new awareness of such thinking. The trajectory between a decorative formalism and the basic expression of the purity of unsullied nature conflicts with the denatured visions which proliferate globally.

The landscape designer Peter Walker pioneered a personal interpretation of Minimalist art as applied to landscape, and in so doing has been able critically to resolve apparent conflicts with aspects of French classical garden design, driven in this case by personal experience of Le Nôtre's great garden at Chantilly. As Walker says:

> Minimalism opens a line of enquiry that may be able to deal with some
> difficult transitions – the loss (or simplification) of craft; transitions from
> traditional materials to synthetics; and extensions of human scale to the
> larger scale (in both space and time) of our mechanically aided modern
> life. Moreover, Minimalism may provide an artistically satisfying approach

Mining machinery at the gold mine on the Dolaucothi Estate near Lampeter in Wales, (c.1950). The alien intrusion of mining works in the landscape

to dealing with two of the most critical environmental problems of our time: dwindling resources and mounting waste.[18]

Walker expresses a particular irony here: that through Minimalism's affinity with classicism there comes recognition of the two sides of nature, the tame and the wild. And yet the ideal surviving from seventeenth-century formalism through classical Modernism remains one of building in a context unconverted from nature, and readily becomes a self-perpetuating myth. Evident recently has been the disengagement of architects from this ideal, of necessity – leading to 'decontextualization' as an inevitable justification for a denatured product, commodified and packaged. As Walker finds, contemporary art is at last legitimized through such historical memories. Ernst Cramer, like Barnett Newman, knew that a straight line is mediated by the surface texture it crosses. The clear 'lines' of Chantilly were threatened by the cult of the Picturesque, yet its designer Le Nôtre eschewed 'pictorialism', as did Smithson and Serra in the 1970s. With truly commendable perception, Walker now extends Minimalism as one route towards the meaningful rehabilitation of contemporary landscape design.

A New Enlightenment

Not surprisingly the continuity of such ancient 'spiritual values', which are often believed to create or harbour the *genius loci* of any given site, remains permanent. Topologies, like morphologies, are more rationally articulated now in terms of such intangibles, by recourse to analyses of the spatial domains of both natural organic structure and also, notably, animal-built structures.[19]

When planning the modern landscape, ancient, aesthetically-driven notions of perspective are nowadays absurdly over-simplistic, even wholly obsolete. New modes of perception are required. This need has occurred because an increasing number of leading architects now demonstrate a wish to relate their buildings to the environment as part of the landscape, rather than simply lodging them within it or positioning them to dominate it, settling for nothing less than a re-invention of the site. More generally, it is important that the shift of paradigm towards 'ecology versus design' is seen to disengage priorities that still propagate a view of landscape that was shaped by classical Modernism.

The Modernist Project: Its Postmodern Revalidation

Traditional concepts of design survived industrialization and, interacting with the philosophy of Modernism, continued to be perceived as models throughout the twentieth century. If we are to revise the parameters of twentieth-century design, adapting them to our own period, we must consider the precedent for Modernist design and the extent to which it has preconditioned the siting of modern architecture within the environment. Such master architects as Frank Lloyd Wright, and more recently Hugo Haring and Hans Scharoun, revealed an intuitive ability to read topologies

Dimitri Pikionis, Acropolis project (1955), looking towards Philopappou Hill. Pikionis successfully pioneered a contemporary approach to hard landscaping

Peter Walker & Partners, Centre for Advanced Sciences and Technology, Hyogo, Japan (1993)

and relate their buildings accordingly. Alvar Aalto designed with no perceptual break between inside and outside.

For landscape architects, too, the extent to which twentieth-century landscape architecture continued to be limited to traditional landscape elements such as water features and plantations of trees connected by 'rides', 'drives' and 'paths', indicates a longstanding, formulaic tradition. Christopher Tunnard's own advocacy that 'modern landscape design is inseparable from the spirit, technique, and development of modern architecture' has to be revalidated by each generation. Public need for contact with nature is increasing rather than diminishing. So the common post-industrial landscape, despite the repeated depredations of high technology in conflict regions, rapidly expands its needs. Industrial sites become new abandoned zones, awaiting the economic capacity and social or political will for restoration. They await the continuation, ironically, of the Modernist project.

New Bearings
'The frontiers of the wild are not easily fixed.'
Simon Schama[20]

If we are to evaluate the scope for new visions of landscape, we must be mindful of Tunnard's belief that the development of landscape design must be inseparable from that of architecture. We must also consider the reality of landscape-contextual primary structures, currently defined purely as architecture. There are some caveats. For example, Ushida Findlay Architects are building (subject to planning permission) a twenty-first century version of the English country house as a seat of power. This proposal engages with the site, but is nonetheless 'denatured', even extra-planetary, in its presumption of the status demanded by the client. Indeed there is no coincidence in the similarity of the 'wings' to the sealed growing tunnels patented for the revolutionary, all-year-round production of cash crops in England. In contrast, Australian architects Denton Corker Marshall (with Chris Blandford Associates as landscape architects) have now brought their Stonehenge Visitor Centre scheme to fruition. The visual impact on the prehistoric site is minimal: this 'abstract form embedded in the landscape' has only the profile of a long, sweeping wall, locking into the rising landform in contour-related folds. Elsewhere, in city blocks, long-prevailing banalities over the 'insertion' of mature trees and velvet grass persist. Examples can be seen not only in Foster and Partners' Swiss-Re city tower in London, but also in Bernard Schumi's Museum of African Art, New York, and Toyo Ito's Mahler 4, Block 5 tower insert with its commodified green trees appearing almost as an afterthought.

Peter Eisenman's City of Culture scheme for Santiago da Compostela (Spain) is, by contrast, very successful. It reconciles figure and ground to incorporate an opera house, auditorium and museum through the medium

The German architect Hans Scharoun (1893–1972) belongs among the Expressionists of post-1918. This sketch, c.1940, displays the perfect synthesis of building into landscape

Alvar Aalto, Villa Mairea at Noormarkku, 1938, where inside and outside become indivisible

of superimposed trace elements. Site topography and medieval city plan are reconciled by Cartesian grid overlay, merging buildings with topography and harmoniously enhancing the existing *genius loci*.

Another success story is by Enric Miralles and Benedetta Tagliabue, who invoked primal landscape notations for the Scottish Parliament, offering homage equally to the ancient volcanic hill adjacent and the neighbouring Holyrood Palace. Some 1.7 hectares of landscaped surroundings incorporate a trail of landscaped walkways harmonized to include local flora and fauna.

For the Tenerife Waterfront, Herzog and de Meuron remind one of the volcanic past, yet by contrast apply 'an artificial landscape like a vessel rather than a piece of architecture'. Low-slung roof surfaces become esplanades along the sea front. Within, the public are both 'embraced' and 'enclosed' by an organic, multi-cellular topological construct.

Toyo Ito's Relaxation Park, Torrevieja, Spain relates sculpturally to lagoons and the sea, using the metaphor of sand dunes. This scheme merges architecture and landscape with complete success, using folding, seashell-like structures which enhance the meaning of the topology. A floating island has been designed for Chongming on 165 square kilometres of silt in the coastal maw of the Yangtse river in China. The British architects Studio BAAD had to find a way to develop a new town on the island without destroying the sensitive ecology. Philip Johnson contributed ideas from New York. There is every indication that a natural habitat will be created here that will enhance Chongming's longstanding image as the 'Garden of Shanghai'.

These buildings will all be completed over the coming decade; they represent a global showcase of diversity, and for the most part suggest that both the architects involved and the landscape designers working in collaboration with them can carry into the future the tendency to harmonize the landscape and its structures without detriment.

There are two small-scale landscape schemes, both by American designers, with which it is appropriate to close this forecast. The landscaped pools, *Landform Ueda* (2002), designed by Charles Jencks for the National Gallery of Modern Art in Edinburgh, represent the fruition of one theorist's longstanding engagement with landscape. Jencks' *House of Elements in Rustic Canyon* (1984) outside Los Angeles celebrates the four elements, Earth, Air, Water and Fire. The design was notable in its search for significant meaning through the combination of house and garden. This was achieved through the design of a series of garden pavilions. Jencks' Edinburgh waterscape is a further representation of the potential of water and open landscape together, albeit carrying meaning at different levels of public and private engagement.

Kathryn Gustafson's competition-winning design for the Memorial to Diana, Princess of Wales at the Serpentine in Hyde Park, London, relies entirely upon the element of water. An oval ring of water engages with the gentle incline of the site, now coursing, now almost still. The result is a design that is accessible to all ages. These remarkable contemporary schemes,

Enric Miralles and Benedetta Tagliabue, Scottish Parliament Building, Edinburgh. Landscape plans that fully merge the building with landscaped site

Charles Jencks' *Landform Ueda*, National Gallery of Modern Art, Edinburgh (2002) marks the return of philosophy to landscape design

both of which will now be realized, suggest a redemption of landscape and its timeless potential to enthral humanity and ennoble its purpose.

New Perceptions
Today there is a sobering note of indictment to many of the earlier Modernist prescriptions, because we are now aware of the full extent to which landscape design had become 'ring-fenced' as a minor activity. However, this situation has resulted in a very open-minded attitude, among both the public and landscape practitioners.

The emergence of a new generation of designers, who came of age as the twentieth century closed, has knocked down the barricades. In the post-war era, the profession lacked any sustained or widespread theoretical discourse. The only exceptions were those cited above. In the 1990s, the French philosopher Jean Baudrillard, a prominent figure in Postmodern criticism, argued that the perceptual boundaries defining the product of conscious thinking have become so far removed from reality that no clear reality or nature exists. All representation is at second hand, though electronically massaged data has its own convinced following. Baudrillard was to say: 'all hold-ups, hijacks and the like are now as it were simulation hold-ups, in the sense that they are inscribed in advance in the decoding and orchestration, anticipated in their mode of presentation and possible consequences within the rituals of the media.'[21]

September 11, 2001 established, in Manhattan, the absurdity of that presumption. Indeed authenticity as a quality seems to be increasing in value after all. Nonetheless, society is becoming more adept at creating virtual events, and landscapes, like buildings, are particularly prone to computerized virtual analysis and re-presentation, even to the extent that increasingly the designed proposal never quite conveys reality.[22]

Filmic memory of place and place-form has, for almost half a century, prefigured these pitfalls of the virtual landscape. The classic masterpiece is *Last Year at Marienbad* (1964) by Alain Resnais, where the figures standing in front of the spa hotel have shadows, and yet the trees formally creating the landscape axis do not, a situation prescient of such dilemmas today. Likewise, Peter Greenaway's *The Draughtsman's Contract* (1984) illustrated the way in which landscape tips the memory towards reality. As part of this transformation in thinking, the filmic process is analogous to the process whereby the design concept for a landscape today is, in theory, derivable from a genetic algorithm which demands that certain key layout parameters are presented in a code script. As with the process of natural mutation and crossover in any natural evolutionary process, a degree of selection is thereby recognized which can predicate eventual form in a coded notation.

Ultimately therefore, landscape designers are no longer seeking a Claudian landscape of tranquillity, but one finely balanced between order and chaos. Increasingly we are becoming aware that the order comes from nature, and the chaos from man. To look at a relevant example, the

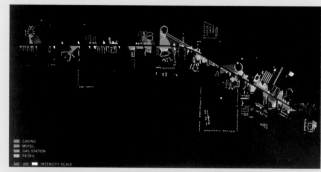

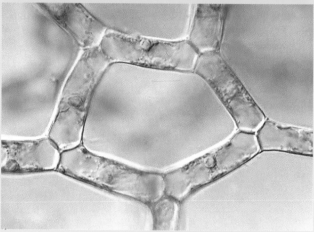

Robert Venturi and Denise Scott-Brown, with Steven Izenow, from *Learning from Las Vegas* (1972). Map of the Las Vegas strip showing intensity of communication, building type and mix

Freshwater algae. Cellular biological structures reveal a microcosmic landscape which has a comparable complexity to the landscape of man

Reversible Destiny City (projected by Arakawa and Madelin Gins, 2000) displays such resolutions with impressive effect. One can even recognize the unsuspecting transfer of the extended phenotype model of Richard Dawkins. The spaces (including the built form) are coded extensions of the human body. The architectural surround is based upon a cellular module that leads to the 'pairing of complex housing together with terrain modules composed of three, five, or seven planes'. In the words of their creators, they 'will rise to form a mound or dip to form a depression'.[22] The housing modules tilt variably, or not at all; in practice, each will boast a landscaped terrace. Inhabitants can move to and fro along linking walkways in a landscaped, green sphere of activity, balanced between the order we crave and the chaos which fascinates us.

Such qualities of indeterminacy in early design models were studied in the 1960s by the French planner Yona Friedman, who focused on habitat, storage, communication and production. Likewise, the work of Peter Cook of the Archigram Group (1974) is notable. Cook's *Sponge City* envisioned a constructed habitat programmed for periodic renewal. The architect Cedric Price also explored the infinite extendibility of the built environment in the context of extreme flexibility and adaptability (1960). Studies in the 1970s of the so-called 'Intelligent Building' sought an 'epistemic autonomy' (i.e. the ability of an organism to improve of its own accord). Such visionary concepts were constrained at the time by the lack of an electronic technology to substantiate their potential on any useful scale. What the landscape community failed to grasp here was the impact of such innovations upon design theory and its implementation, whether applicable to architecture or to landscape.

Architects ultimately took the lead in such thinking, in a number of cases. In a conference at the Architectural Association in 1996, architecture was proclaimed by John Frazer as possessing 'an open relationship with the environment … to generate new forms and structure … not a static picture of being, but a dynamic picture of becoming, and unfolding, in a direct analogy with a description of the natural world.'[23]

If, in this natural 'landscape', the twin phenomena of self-assembly and self-organization can lead to the construction of large 'molecular assemblies' and supra-molecular 'arrays' with both form and function, the implications for the new landscape are sufficiently interesting to mobilize new discourse within the landscape profession. If it is architects who are today criticized for speculating overmuch about the future of landscape, they have nonetheless thrown open the gates to inspirational new design for all engaged with the environment as a whole. Meanwhile, the cyclical debate between ecological and aesthetic or stylistic priorities will continue, and will be periodically resolved.

A whole range of inspirational ideas have in fact been made available by artists, such as Robert Smithson, as we have seen above. The influence of painters on landscape and garden design was strong in the period of the

Peter Cook (Archigram), Sponge City, 1974

Reversible Destiny City, Tokyo Bay, by Arakawa and Madeline Gins (2000)

Enlightenment. But today, the modern landscape has been dramatically re-conceived through the Land Art installations that have proliferated since the 1980s. They have allowed a new reverence for nature, and new perceptions for implanting man's work on the earth. A pastoral mood is now prevalent. It is the prerequisite of landscape designers acting for society at large, to embrace and rationalize such modern theoretical frontiers. In so doing, they will maximize the potential of earthly 'Pairideaeza'. For Paradise was always an option, to be grasped, not lost.

Notes

1 Max Bill uses the term 'product-form' to express the tendency for industrial design objects to be defined both by operating constraints and ergonomic functions. Frampton (*Architectural Review*, October 1999, pp.75–80) borrowed the term, comparing it with 'place-form' and drawing attention to the 'high-tech' architects 'who have reinterpreted the craft of building in terms of modern productive methods [and who] have in effect been engaged in creating buildings which are largely determined by production methods' (p.78). This tendency is substantially more developed today than it was even in 1999. Frampton also offers an alternative definition of place-form: 'The foundational, topographic element that in one way or another is cast into the ground as a heavyweight site component that offers a form of quite literal resistance to the lightweight, productional superstructure poised on top of it.'

2 The Architectural Association held a symposium (17 March, 1995) entitled 'The Recovery of Landscape', chaired by Alan Balfour, followed by a Royal Academy, London Symposium on the 18th of March, 1995, chaired by this author, subsequently published as *Landscape Transformed* (ed. Michael Spens) in 1996. These two separate but co-ordinated events essentially broke new ground, focusing on current works built by 1995. This somewhat outdated two previous published surveys, Sutherland Lyall, *Designing the New Landscape* (1991) and Michael Lancaster, *The New European Landscape* (1986). Both were marginally updated in new editions by 1995. Marc Treib, *Modern Landscape Architecture: a Critical Review* (1993) provided a useful appraisal. But there remains no comprehensive survey and analysis of the critical shift in design emphasis that occurred over the past decade. More recent publications in Europe and America, while giving indications of the directions new thinking follows, have done little more to provide clear guidance

3 Later, it is clear that the ethos of Calvinism and Lutheran thinking had profoundly affected developments in both science and philosophy from the seventeenth century onwards. An eighteenth-century strand of obsession with the ruins of antiquity occurred in parallel with the newly expanding fields of learning in geology and astrology. Of major significance as a motivating force was the science-based aspect of the Enlightenment. This was the search for a major universal truth linking past and future parameters of time, upsetting the immutability of the classical heritage

4 Sir James Hall is fully discussed by Joseph Rykwert in *On Adam's House in Paradise: The Idea of the Primitive Hut in Architectural History*, New York: Museum of Modern Art, 1972. Hall's romantic theory was, as Rykwert states, 'comtemptuously dismissed' in turn by Friedrich von Schlegel in his *Works*, Vol. 5, Paris, 1794, p.194

5 *Origine de tous les cultes: ou le religion universelle*, Paris, 1794

6 *Letters from Petrarch*, selected and translated by M Bishop, Bloomington, IN: Indiana University Press, 1966, p.152

7 David H Solkin, *Richard Wilson: The Landscape of Reaction*, London: Tate Gallery, 1982. This exhibition, curated by Solkin, applied a fresh perspective to Wilson's painting and relations to clients, purveying a patrician notion of rural life. For a full discussion see ch. 1, 'The Happy Rural Life', pp.22–34

8 Thomas Whateley, *Observations on Modern Gardening*, London, second edition, 1770

9 Gilbert Highet, *Poets in a Landscape*, London: Pelican, 1959. Provides a full description of the work of Virgil and others against their historical and geographical background

10 Dorothy Stroud, *Capability Brown*, London: Faber, 1975 (first edition 1950). Lancelot 'Capability' Brown is fully documented by Stroud, who selected Kimberley Hall, Wymondham, Norfolk, on account of 'the enlarging of the lake to some 28 acres'. This 1763 scheme preceded that for Melton Constable, also in Norfolk (but minus water feature), by a year. See also John Phibbs, 'The Survival of Lancelot "Capability" Brown', in *Landscape Transformed*, ed. Michael Spens, London: Academy Editions, 1995, pp.38–43

11 The project by Danil Fedorovich Fridman (1887–1950) for Green City (1930) provided dynamic and static leisure zones of harmonious forest parkland; and that by Mikhail Zhirov (1898–1977) for a Park of Culture and Leisure, also in Moscow (1929), drew landscape and planting dramatically within the built 'ring'. But these were rare examples

12 Camillo Schneider, 'Die Gartenbau Ausstellung (Zuga)', *Gartenschonheit*, 10, 1933, p.199

13 Peter Latz, originally quoted in 'Lifescapes', the introduction to Udo Weilacher, *Visionary Gardens: Modern Landscapes by Ernst Cramer*, Basel: Birkhäuser, 2001, p.9

14 The Greek architect Dimitri Pikionis bore out such ideas in his design for the area close to the Acropolis.

15 At Salt Lake, Utah, Smithson drew upon the native legend that the lake where the spiral was constructed was in fact bottomless and connected to the Pacific. The timeless quality aspired to by Smithson unwittingly became evidence for a last rite, as the lake water level rose unpredictably to absorb this symbol of a generation's act of homage to nature. The sculpture has, however, resurfaced during 2002

16 Colin Rowe, *The Architecture of Good Intentions: Towards a Possible Retrospect*, London: Academy Editions, 1994, pp.111–13 and 117

17 For reference to Robert Smithson see Yve-Alain Bois, 'A Picturesque Stroll around Clara-Clara', *October, The First Decade, 1976–1986*, ed. Michelson, Krauss, Crimp and Copjec, Cambridge, MA: MIT Press, 1987, pp. 342–72. See also Robert Smithson, 'Frederick Law Olmsted and the Dialectical Landscape', *The Writings of Robert Smithson*, ed. Nancy Holt, New York: New York University Press, 1979, pp. 118–19

18 Peter Walker, 'Minimalist Gardens', *Space Design (SD), Monthly Journal of Art and Architecture*, Tokyo, July 1994, p.25

19 In the late 1960s the scientist Richard Dawkins developed the idea of 'the extended phenotype'. But only latterly have research scientists given full attention to the notion of physiological perspective which such theories entail. The study of the same natural phenomena, the organisms pursued by D'Arcy Thompson, has led today to the process of molecular and biological research that offers a clear bearing upon the morphology of the modern landscape. New technology enables dramatically closer analysis of such phenomena. The 'realm' of an organism is now considered to be indivisible in associational terms, for the given species, from the organism itself. This inevitably has a direct bearing upon the spatial concept of landscape. The neo-Darwinian school of revisionary theory here loses interest in the idea of the organism itself, and feeds vigorously on the information emerging about the very gene structures that dictate life

20 'For it seems to me that neither the frontiers between the wild and the cultivated, nor those that lie between the past and the present, are so easily fixed.' Simon Schama, *Landscape and Memory*, London: Fontana Press, 1996, p.574

21 Jean Baudrillard, 'America', *Simulacra and Simulations*, trans. S F Glaser, Michigan: University of Michigan Press, 1984, pp.12–13, 91–2

22 Arakawa and Madeline Gins, *Architectural Design*, vol. 68, no. 11/12, Nov–Dec 1998, pp.42–5

23 John H Frazer, *An Evolutionary Architecture*, London: Architectural Association Press, 1996, p.21

Parkland

The thirty or so case studies in this book have been structured into four distinct, if overlapping, groups. This section includes recent, large-scale designed environments, partially or wholly completed, in widely differing geographical contexts.

Such projects are led by landscape architects, albeit on an inter-disciplinary basis, with engineers as well as artists often involved. The eighteenth-century park at Castletown Cox Park, Ireland (2002), recently recovered from near-dereliction by new owners and developed in an imaginative and scholarly manner by Colvin and Moggridge, contrasts with Jacqueline Osty's Parc St Pierre, Amiens, France (1994), a brilliant retrieval of the historical periphery of a cathedral city, knitted together with remarkable creative skill.

Among other large-scale landscape projects is Itsuko Hasegawa's Niigata-city. This example of a waterside leisure park consists of an archipelago-based integration of bridges, gardens and a performing arts centre on the largest island. This category encompasses emergent historical parks, such as the landscape of memory in the Peace Park on the Gallipoli Peninsula in Turkey. Conceived by John Lonsdale, Nynke Joustra and Steve Reid, with Volker Ulrich, it is as yet only partially realized. Here, systematic archaeological research of key areas across the 330 square kilometres has generated a choreography of routes in former areas of conflict. This memory landscape makes a contrast to more conventional cemeteries, such as the German military cemetery of the Passo la Futa, Italy (Oesterlen and Rossow, 1967), a masterpiece of architectonic Land Art, and a worthy precedent. Equally, no history of twentieth-century landscape should overlook the British equivalent, the superbly planted war cemeteries of the Imperial War Graves Commission, as at Cassino. The Polish cemetery at Cassino is equally impressive.

The park of memories is an important category. Within it we may also find the work of Gigon and Guyer, recently completed at Kalkriese, Germany. This recalls dramatically, and in an entirely Minimalist contemporary mode, a definitive victory against the Romans, along the key landscape feature, the Teutoburger Wald in North Germany.

Increasingly, parkland includes major public schemes developed in mitigation of major despoliation through industrial, military or long-running contamination. Danadjieva and Koenig Associates' West Point Wastewater Treatment Plant, Seattle is a fine example of a design that counters the visual effects of effluent processes. Industrial blight on a massive scale is successfully mitigated by Peter Latz's work at Emscher Park, Duisburg-Nord, Germany. The precedent on the regional scale for parklands embodies research methodologies evolved by Ian McHarg in his pioneering *Plan for the Valleys* (1963) by Wallace McHarg Associates, covering a substantial area north west of Baltimore. More recent work on sustainability came from the late John Lyle (1934–98) who produced a seminal study entitled *Regenerative Design for Sustainable Development in California.* The work by Fred Phillips

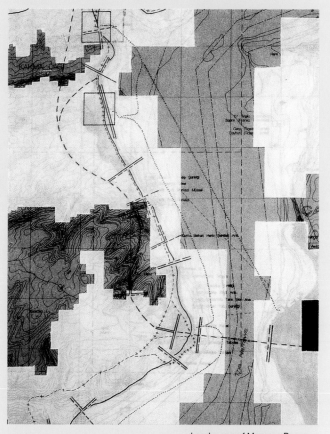

Landscape of Memory, Peace Park, Gallipoli, Turkey, by Big House: John Lonsdale, Nynke Joustra, Steve Reid, with Voiker Ulrich, competition entry (1988). A mnemonic landscaped memorial park under current development

in recovery and regeneration in Yuma East Wetlands, Colorado River, best demonstrates the growth and practical application of such principles on a large scale.

Parkland forms a useful category of landscape architecture. While acknowledging an essential Enlightenment precedent, it also encompasses the impressive development of the public, urban park that evolved during the nineteenth and twentieth centuries. The idea of the park is rooted partly in the medieval concept of sport or leisure. Areas of countryside were reserved in medieval times for the chase, for hunting animals on horseback or on foot. In due course, however, the park took on another role. It served as an antidote to the poor public sanitation and overcrowding in cities, conditions that brought with them a permanent threat of epidemic or plague. Parks then were literally, as they remain psychologically, the 'lungs' of the city.

In the later twentieth century, landscape designers have increasingly sought to capitalize upon existing water features such as rivers, lakes, pools and coastline; where these have not existed, they have been created artificially, to great effect. The idea of parkland, then, bears witness in England to the important post-war designs of Geoffrey Jellicoe, and indeed of Sylvia Crowe, both pioneers of the twentieth-century landscape profession.

The park at Ronneby Sanatorium, Sweden, by Sven Ingvar Andersson (1987) evolved within the more constricted field of garden art. Andersson has frequently worked with artists in Denmark, returning to his native Sweden to achieve a masterly recreation of a decayed 35-hectare manorial park at Ronneby, constructing new lakes with definite, almost geometric shorelines.

By definition, the 'parkland' landscape designs included in this section tend to be primarily the work of professional landscape architects, given the substantial investment involved. These projects, selected from a wide range, reveal criteria for design which essentially reflect post-industrial thinking and an awareness of ecological and sustainability factors, issues which were not pronounced until the 1990s. Aesthetically and philosophically, such schemes reveal the designers' awareness of the elemental relationship of humanity to fragile earth, and of the vulnerability of natural flora and fauna on site. But increasingly, too, the influence of Land Artists becomes prevalent. As Andersson claimed at Ronneby, the sculptors Richard Serra and Christo gave him inspiration. The manipulation of space itself, rather than of objects in space, remains critical here, but there has to be a corresponding perception in the public eye. As Andersson was asked about the large new expanses of water he created: 'Ronneby is a wonderful park, but what is it that you built there?'

Bet Figueras' Barcelona Botanic Gardens fulfils the essence of the public park while providing a long-term horticultural template. In both instances the entertainment and leisure needs of a discerning public are intelligently catered for, witness to a tradition of botanic gardens stretching back to the Enlightenment.

Parkland

Castletown Cox
County Kilkenny, Ireland, 2001

Colvin & Moggridge

The landscape plan as reconceived by Colvin and Moggridge. The house is right of centre

The epitome of an efflorescent, eclectic, national style of architecture can often be found in paraphrased form well beyond the territories where it was first established. Castletown Cox, County Kilkenny, is a case in point, as much for its architecture as for its immediate surroundings. The house at Castletown celebrates the English Enlightenment, and yet it is an intriguing agglomeration of English and Italian elements, enlivened by the full sway of the Anglo-Irish Ascendancy. The Franco-Italian architect-engineer Davisco d'Arcot came to Ireland in the mid-eighteenth century. Emerging as Davis Duckart, he appears to have readily assimilated the ways of his new country, but not at the expense of his Italian cultural grounding.

Duckart's first major country house in Ireland was Kilshanig, begun in 1765 for a banking family, while Castletown seems to have commenced in 1770. Both houses reveal a similar plan of main block, L-shaped wings and twin-domed side-pavilions. Clearly Duckart was familiar with the classical British mansions as documented by the Palladian architect Colen Campbell in his *Vitruvius Britannicus*, published before 1725, nearly two generations earlier. There appears to be a formal correspondence between the layout of Castletown and that of Castle Howard by Sir John Vanbrugh. The twin cupolas, however, seem to reflect those by James Gibbs for the towers first designed by Colen Campbell at Houghton Hall, Norfolk in the 1720s, incorporated after Campbell's death. Familiarity with the architecture there, whether first-hand or from a secondary source, is suggested too in the siting of the house, which shows an awareness of the ideas of Lancelot 'Capability' Brown who had affected important changes at Vanbrugh's Blenheim Palace from 1763, and perhaps earlier at Croome Court. These and other developments in England by Brown reinforced the concept of an oblique rather than centrally axial approach to a grand house through its park, as appropriate to the English eighteenth-century house. But at Castletown Cox there had never been a park.

When Hal Moggridge and Mark Darwent of Colvin and Moggridge were commissioned at Castletown Cox, they were obliged effectively to start from scratch, although the landscape clearly offered what Brown had always referred to as 'the capability' to be developed in a suitable vein. They and their client found this quality all around. So with a masterly combination of contemporary landscape design skills and historical scholarship, they have, after two and a quarter centuries, simply brought the scheme for the park to fruition.

Castletown now offers a completely unbroken sequence of views, through the approach, on arrival and on entry to the building. While the exterior detailing by Duckart may be described as somewhat eccentrically Italian, the interior reveals the skilful mastery of the distinguished Irish plasterer Patrick Osborne. The overall result, with its rich rococo plasterwork and intentionally overscaled joinery, is truly Irish and without inhibition. Castletown can be described as an integrated masterpiece. The new owners, Mr and Mrs George Magan, have set about restoring these qualities now that the surrounding park has been reunited with the house. The majority of the original demesne has been bought back, and 203 hectares (500 acres) of parkland now complement the house. Already some 80,000 trees have been planted here. The original, somewhat detached, lake and the canal made by Duckart, who had previously trained as an engineer, have both been dredged out. A long, Brownian ha-ha has been built to fulfil its traditional role, that of invisibly protecting the regenerated gardens from the cattle which now graze in the park.

Colvin and Moggridge are perhaps the longest-established and most distinguished British landscape architects practising today. Their portfolio contains outstanding examples of both contemporary landscape design and recovery and restoration projects. Early in his career, Hal Moggridge worked with Sir Geoffrey Jellicoe (1900–96). He has maintained an approach grounded in Modernist principles, and his application of these principles is characterized by scholarly discipline, well-founded and exacting research and the use of a substantial database. At Castletown the challenge was an entirely contemporary one: how was the 'capability' needed to complete the total project to be reconciled with problems posed by the complexity of the present-day planning legislation, expanding local commercial forestry provisions, and the general lack of co-ordination of no less than three relevant local development plans impinging upon the Castletown area? Hal Moggridge and Mark Darwent assiduously worked through such problems in order to complete the project, but the time-scale for overall completion was inevitably protracted as a consequence.

A broad view of the landscape shows that Castletown Cox commands the central plain of the River Suir from a natural knoll. The views are dramatic, to the Slievenamon Mountain to the west, towards lower hills south across the valley, and towards the ancient Comeragh Mountains in the far distance. The local sandstone and unpolished blue-grey Kilkenny marble of the external elevations stand out in this Arcadian landscape, while the south-western axiality of the house has been tempered, allowing the broader visual envelope of the environment to be more authentically experienced. Some of the new planting will be dedicated to enhancing the sequence of views on the new approach, and to blocking out new rural development where it impacts

View to aperture beneath canopy

View to Slievenamon

Castletown Cox

Right: Castletown Cox, the main, south facade

Below: View from the house, down the new avenue of trees to the mountains

Opposite, above: The existing park enhanced

Opposite, below: The original lake excavated by Duckart in the 1770s

unnecessarily on views from the house. These are a constantly shifting performance of Irish mist, with grey, blue and ochre tones animating the ancient panorama that remains. The house had been shut in by more recently planted trees, but these have now been felled. A great bonus is the survival of the east pool, really a small lake, and the canal that has fed it ever since Duckart first dug it out.

The western approach drive has been slightly re-aligned. This represents a radical improvement as it maximizes the sequence of views to the house. An important beech avenue to the west has been recognized within the master plan, and an oval pool suggested by the client has been inserted on the axis between the ha-ha and the south-west front. Water already plays a significant role at Castletown, and this will be increased by the pools and bridge planned for the new south-western approach drive. The new bridge close to the south park encourages the visitor to pause briefly and experience a slightly oblique frontal view of the house. This drama refers lightly to the concept of the 'Sublime' as much as to the 'beautiful', as then developed by the Irish philosopher Edmund Burke (who had in later life found some of his thinking borne out in the work of 'Capability' Brown). Burke (1729–97), a Dubliner, was a contemporary of Castletown's creator, Michael Cox, Archbishop of Cashel, and was from 1761–5 intellectually and politically active in Dublin, and Private Secretary to the Secretary for Ireland. Such aesthetic theories would, as in England, have been prevalent.

For the visitor today, the dramatic experience of approaching Castletown Cox is enhanced by the superb sweep of the continuation of the drive as it first commands an axial view of the whole house, and then runs closer to its terminus on the north-eastern forecourt. In the foreground, groups of garden trees have been planted to mark the transition in scale around the building, and to provide a frame for the existing planting. The sense of almost total enclosure at the entrance (to the north) is maintained. The combination of traditional ha-ha, lawns, parterres and paving, flower gardens, longer grass, bulbs and spring flowers, and screen planting is carefully orchestrated by Colvin and Moggridge and their client to further the mutual enhancement of house and landscape. Supporting agricultural land will now be properly organized to avoid over-grazing damaging the ecology, and to provide natural winter fodder.

Hal Moggridge and his partner-in-charge Mark Darwent have ensured that this house is at last the focus of a wholly impressive environment. History is re-postulated with a contemporary rigour combined with a skilfully applied understanding of the historical context of place and time.

Parkland

Parc St Pierre
Amiens, France, 1996

Jacqueline Osty

Parc St Pierre

Parc St Pierre

Opposite, above: Overall view of the site

Opposite, below: Overall landscape plan and sections across site

In 1990 the city of Amiens, the regional capital of the ancient province of Picardy, decided that its historical past was being increasingly overlooked. Tourist brochures tended to focus largely, and perhaps obsessively, upon its role in the First World War. The council selected an area on the north side of the city that was slipping into dereliction, and made it the subject of a landscape design competition for a new park. Their aim was both to regenerate a forgotten area, and restore a sense of Amiens' traditional identity as an economic and religious centre. The chosen area offered a unique opportunity to create a new, accessible space in the shadow of the cathedral, and to revive a pedestrian route into the city from the north. The catalyst was water, a predominant yet unexploited asset, for the site was linked to and bounded by the River Somme and its tributary system.

The young French landscape designer Jacqueline Osty finally emerged as the winner of the competition, against an international field of 48 entries. Osty had been trained by Michel Corajoud at the École Nationale Supérieure du Paysage in Versailles. One of her primary strengths proved to be a closely detailed knowledge of the city and the site itself. She rapidly realized that water was the key to solving the problem, and that it existed already in various emergent and declining roles across the site.

Amiens has a long history as a satin-weaving community, and the mills had influenced the management of water in the city since the Middle Ages. The River Somme ran along the boundary of the site to the south. The Abbey also exerted an important influence on the cultivated lands close by, as the monks used to license plots and manage irrigation. Two important riverside areas, called the Étang St Pierre and the Étang Rivery, were divided from each other by a raised highway, the Boulevard de Beauville. The Étang St Pierre was popular with anglers, and the Étang Rivery lay alongside an area of vegetable plots known as the Hortillonages, created over several centuries by the silting up of the banks of the Somme and the nearby River Arve. Land of this kind once accounted for up to a thousand hectares (2,500 acres) around Amiens. In 1990 only 15 hectares (40 acres) at most remained. These vegetable gardens, served by well-maintained dykes linked to communally operated canals, were once very important. A seamless progression of cash crops was delivered to market by small vessels like punts, with up to three different crops produced each year. The council was determined to preserve a remnant of this tradition for posterity. There had always been conflict between the interests of the satin mill owners and those of the vegetable growers, as the mills demanded minimum fixed levels of water, and these tended to flood the vegetable beds.

This problem was resolved at the time of the French Revolution in favour of the smallholders. Today, the 'Association pour la Protection et la Sauvegarde du Site et de l'Environnement' has responsibility for securing the operability of the canals and dykes and, equally significantly here, for preserving the social, cultural and ecological history of the site.

Jacqueline Osty phased development carefully across two main areas. Firstly, she dealt with the 15 hectares (37 acres) already owned by the city. Secondly, she reconsidered the 6 or so hectares remaining in private ownership. The majority of this private land was occupied by the Hortillonages. In both areas water was the catalytic element that would knit together the various uses planned for the site. This involved a carefully evolved hydraulic engineering plan, to ensure that a hierarchy of watercourses remained active. The Étang St Pierre was preserved as more of a lake than a swamp, while retaining aspects of the natural ecology of reeds and rushes that had stabilized the edge of the site for centuries. Osty also provided wooden jetties to facilitate fishing at the water's edge. A major solid walkway, the Promenade du Jours, was created at right angles to the highway. Massive embankments and steps marked the conjunction of the Promenade and the level of the highway, which became a viewing platform.

The bulk and spire of Amiens Cathedral dominates the view to the south. Osty envisaged the Parc St Pierre as a repository for the city's memories, its very sense of place and identity literally enhanced by the shadow of the cathedral. In the northern sector of the park, three water courses establish a kind of web, one running from the tributary, the other two coursing gently from the lake itself. Gardens of lilies are positioned above these. To the south, the flow of the Bras Baraban tributary establishes a clear boundary which is crossed by a pedestrian bridge. Allotments have been re-introduced on the approach to the Somme, each accessible from the towpath.

Completing the two parts of the scheme, the Étang Rivery to the East is joined to the Étang St Pierre by the ingenious use of a pre-existing canal tunnel under the highway. A lightweight pedestrian bridge has been inserted through the tunnel, spanning the canal. The Étang St Pierre, with its lush water gardens, marks the gradual movement southwards via paths which offer varying views of the cathedral, becoming gradually less formal in character as they approach the Somme. The Promenade des Jours, as the main pedestrian axis, is marked out clearly by a newly planted line of plane trees. The whole water landscape opens up southwards, criss-crossed by paths of wooden decking

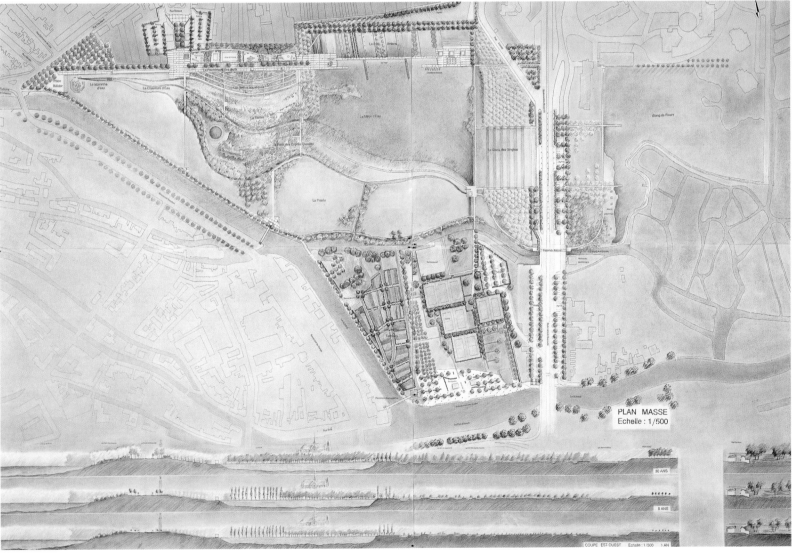

PLAN MASSE
Echelle : 1/500

COUPE EST-OUEST   Echelle : 1/500   1 AN

30 ANS

8 ANS

Right: Pathway elevated across marshlands, past shaded pavilion

Opposite, above left: Marsh ponds with willow and alder closely planted to recreate historical conditions for the Hortillonage

Below left: Water-lily gardens established on the south side of the Promenade des Jours

Below right: Promenade des Jours, looking towards the cathedral

which sometimes lead off to the remaining marshlands, giving privacy and encouraging exploration. The calm expanse of the Étang St Pierre reflects the cathedral.

Osty has been decisive and has maintained the totality of her concept. Where she has needed to employ specialists, such as water engineers or architects, she has kept control. The architects Maurer and Orgi were brought in specifically to design a metal pergola and arbour, creating a threshold in a key location on the promenade. The planting plan was also highly specific to the environment intended, with a concentration on trees and plants rather than flowers. Colour has, however, been a critical ingredient. Osty has chosen her species for practicality and for effect. On the steep slope bordering the highway she has planted *Gingko biloba* on a grid scheme, reducing the impact of the embankment. The American Swamp Cypress (*Taxodium distichum*) is another exotic species that has been imported, and proves admirably suited to the ecology of the Étang. It has been established close to the water in every case, and forms a further wooded component, mediating between marsh and open meadow. To give seasonal colour, poplar, willow, bird

cherry and the ubiquitous alder have been planted. Osty has ensured the stabilization of existing Lombardy poplars and white willows through careful husbandry. An added bonus in season, too, is the riot of colour produced by the varieties of vegetables grown on the allotments south-west of the park.

In reviewing Osty's achievement, and the way in which she has fulfilled the intelligent aspirations of the Amiens City Council, one becomes aware of an orchestration of events. Osty acknowleged the catalytic value of water at a very early stage, using it in a variety of formal and less formal ways. This helped to develop a clear structure of routes and paths, allowing pedestrians to move across the site along carefully established routes. The paths evoke a sense of freedom, allowing one to move at a chosen pace in a wide and varied range of directions. Not to be underestimated either is the extent to which the landscape designer has recast the very identity of a whole city, reminding us of its past and reassuring its inhabitants of their cultural heritage and its future scope. Osty has provided cultural continuity, meaning and poetry.

Right: Overview across the park from the steep incline of the Boulevard Beauville

Below: Bridge connecting the park with the town

Opposite, all: *Amiens, ville verte, Amiens, ville bleu* ('Amiens is a green city and a blue city'). Traditionally recognized as a cathedral city, Amiens is set in a landscape of horticulture and water in a variety of different guises. As these pictures show, Osty has provided many new and varied combinations of both

Parkland

Emscher Park
Duisburg-Nord, Germany, 1993–2001
Peter Latz & Partners

Opposite, above left: Emscher Park, showing the highly developed density of the locality when the industrial facilities were still in operation

Opposite, above right: Emscher Park, raw industrial material woven through with landscape elements

Opposite, centre and below left: The industrial raw material. Footbridges are re-activated: an archaeology of metal structures. A 'zone' of abandoned objects is publicly re-activated

Opposite, below right: The Piazza Metallica pays physical homage to the history of the site as a steel refinery

Emscher Park, in Germany's twentieth-century industrial heartland, remains for landscape architect Peter Latz the project in which a whole range of issues came together, forming the premise for nothing less than a dramatic revision of the whole ethos of landscape architecture. Such preoccupations had already come to the fore in Peter Latz and Partners' previous project for the Hafeninsel (Harbour Island) in Saarbrucken, carried out between 1985 and 1989. The 9-hectare (22-acre) site near the city centre was once the location of a Saarbrucken coal dock. The entire site was infilled with bomb debris and random rubble. Latz viewed the wartime bombing that had created this urban desert as historical in its own right and set about consolidating, rather than seeking to remove, the impacted surfaces, undrained pools and developing ecology that had sprung up in the following two generations. In the process, a deeper history of industrial residues was revealed that could have been lost for ever. In this way, Latz linked the industrial history of the Hafeninsel site with the city's current transportation infrastructure, reconceived public gardens and their pedestrian paths, and identified axes of visual reconciliation.

If the Hafeninsel site can be decribed as a twentieth-century construct, Emscher Park emerges as very much the 'Park of the Twenty-First Century' in Latz's plans. While at Hafeninsel he established what was essentially an 'open' park concept, embracing the idea of continuous change and development, at Emscher Park this opportunity did not exist. The massive former iron and steel works of Duisburg Meiderich was littered with an archaeology of seemingly immovable heavy industrial plant. The flora and fauna of half a century had grown across this artificial topography prolifically and without constraint. Certain rare species had emerged, and the ecology had expanded largely without any further intrusion by man. The archaeology itself comprised of massive blast furnaces, towering chimneys and cranes, abandoned railway track, shunting and parking sheds, iron bridges and colossal ore heaps: a legacy of the production of nearly 40 million tonnes of high quality pig iron. The immediate question, of course, was whether all this dereliction could possibly be converted safely and economically into anything approaching a leisure park, maximizing the fullest future potential for all 230 hectares (570 acres) of available wasteland.

As at Hafeninsel, Peter Latz imposed a rudimentary landscape planning grid over the site, which enabled him to establish the underlying pattern of things. In this way he identified three templates of physical reality: a water regime consisting of pools and linking canals, a *bahnpark* or rail area of raised walkways, and a series of long, elevated promenades. Across these elements the fractures, elisions and slippages in contour and interactions of natural geology persisted. The whole apparatus, however, was an artificial construct, and Latz found himself having to apply a fantasy narrative to these depressing relics. He adopted an approach not so very different from the speculations of Sir Arthur Evans at Knossos in Crete (1899–1935). However, he was able to activate the archaeology freely, as in a child's mind, rather than perpetrate a deception about revered archaeological remains with the *gravitas* of fact. In an interview, Latz compared his 'fiction-writing' of a necessary narrative with 'a falcon circling a mountain'.

Although he does not seek to replicate the ideals of the Italian Renaissance garden, Latz admits to cross-referencing Emscher Park with the monsters of Bomarzo. He recognized the threat industry posed to ecology throughout the nineteenth and twentieth centuries, and how the satanic foreboding of the Emscher Park metal monsters pursues humanity unchecked into the twenty-first century.

Emscher Park is imbued with a new understanding of nature. Latz began his career in horticulture, developing professionally as an urban planner before moving into landscape design. At Emscher Park the idea of nature is not confused with that of landscape. For Latz, nature is usually something divorced from landscape: landscape exists as a cultural phenomenon, while nature is a self-determining force. He has created an entirely artificial metal landscape between the furnaces at Emscher Park. Named Piazza Metallica, it serves as a meeting point for visitors. The Piazza also draws attention to two aspects of the nature of metal. The industrial infrastructure reminds the visitor of the creation, over many generations, of the solid, hardened product, a process that demands temperatures of some 1,300 degrees centigrade. Metal is also present in an eroded form, deprived by time of its molten, energizing force. In Latz's view this process is as much a feature of nature as, for example, the carefully located trees and planting of conventional landscape design.

The *Gleisharfe* (the Rail Harp) is another feature of the site. It notates the interweaving of repetitively disposed rail track, so each second track runs downwards with the

Right: New, pedestrian-scale steps and walkways are threaded between large-scale, redundant structures of the industrial past

Below: The fern garden and a construction detail in the fern garden

Opposite: The Cowperplatz

Right: Wind vane and canal.
Windpower is used to clean and
to transport water around the
site

Opposite, above: Pedestrian
bridges cross clearwater canals,
which are fed by rainwater

Opposite, below: View over
Emscher Park to Duisburg-Nord,
revealing the recovery of
natural, random vegetation over
abandoned ground, giving a
wholly unexpected green
backdrop

intervening lines running upwards. This Railway Park was
readily conceived by Latz in the very earliest stages of
design, when confronted by this curiously interesting
structure as found. Indeed, the apparent resemblance of the
construct with some forms of deliberately contrived Land Art
does not escape his notice. Furthermore, Latz will argue that
the recognition of such artificial manifestations of
engineering, crossing over the imposed delineations
between architecture and landscape, just go to emphasize
that the divisions are largely redundant in the context of
modern landscape design.

By contrast, and more conventionally, Latz has also
created a circular fern garden within the complex. He has
located a series of small planted areas in the former coal
bunkers, a structure providing the seclusion of the Medieval
hortus conclusus. Overhead a great wheel rotates, providing
spectacular water circulation within the general plan. Where
the gigantic muller bunkers rise, Latz interposes a mood of
irony, providing a simple cross to mark 'Monte Thyssino', a
parody of the bombed wartime monastery site of Monte
Cassino, and a pun on the name of Europe's greatest steel
manufacturer. At Duisburg-Nord, European historical
memories are very much brought into play. Aware of all this,
Latz has created a great landscape monument reflecting the
real issues inherited by the leisure society of the twenty-first
century.

Parkland

**Yokohama Portside Park
Yokohama, Japan, 1999**

Hiroki Hasegawa

Right: Overview of model (detail) showing the careful integration of landscape berms with the built form

Far right: At the water's edge, carefully detailed and integrated barriers of different material ensure safety

Below: Pathways built from setts

Opposite: General site plan, revealing the integration of components with new plantations

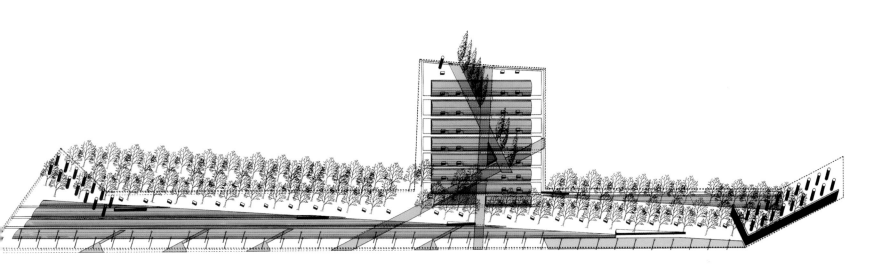

Yokohama is one of many industrial cities and ports in Japan in which the authorities are seeking to develop the waterfront as part of the new concept of a city zone of mixed-use development. In time, this will entirely replace the obsolete urban infrastructure, a relic of past misconceptions. In Yokohama the new waterfront is intended to be a park in its own right. Hiroki Hasegawa has utilized various established landscape conventions, familiar in both western and eastern landscape history. Cobbles and setts as pavings are sensitively deployed and steel elements, wooden decking, brick plazas, lawns and mounds as well as native vegetation are used to evoke the memory of the area's historic past, while opening up a meaningful future. A kind of landscape mosaic of events and earlier predispositions is thus accrued. In particular, the use of various reflective elements aids the development of visual interest, even excitement.

The entire park is made up of sequential layers. Earthwork berms are designed to run the full length of the site, parallel to the waterfront. The designer has evolved a concise form of visual language that mixes characteristics of the ocean with those of the city.

Hiroki Hasegawa has marked the main entrance to the park with grass mounds, some moulded regularly in pattern and others cut through, diminishing in size as they reach down to the waterline. A double row of elms, some 400 metres (436 yards) in length, helps mark out the full length of the waterfront promenade, and timber decking pushes out over the water at regular intervals. The lack of a clear boundary to the site is deliberate. In Hasegawa's own words, he has created 'a garden without boundaries'. Natural vegetation such as reeds and native grasses has been encouraged to spread, still protected by pre-cast concrete blocks which retain the soil and reduce the impact of waves. This is an active waterfront where children can freely roam and the whole system of routes, paths and decks encourages both games and rest and reflection. The edge of the water is marked in places by well-designed, low-level wooden fencing.

Innumerable cities now cherish their recovered waterfronts, first abandoned by shipping and docking concerns, now retrieved for a useful, more human engagement by local inhabitants. As time goes on the natural vegetation will proliferate, re-establishing historic profiles that would have existed before industrialization.

At Osawana Kenko Fureai Park (1999), Hiroki Hasegawa undertook a similar process to that at Yokohama, although on a somewhat smaller scale. Working with Studio on Site, he made a careful study of the existing and pre-existing land-use patterns. From this information he evolved a reflection of the historic agricultural regime that had previously existed.

In 1993 the same partnership designed the Natori Cultural Hall South Garden. There they conceived a symbolic forest at the centre of the scheme, where abstracted rows of trees were invaded by randomly-scattered species. Here lawn mounds were developed to create a counter-rhythm to the 'forest'.

The sequential development of Hiroki Hasegawa's work over this six-year period demonstrates a successful and evolving philosophy of landscape design which recognizes the interaction of relatively formalized elements with more random planting.

Opposite, above left and below: Longitudinal berms, with granite sett paths between, run on axis with the water's edge, providing areas for play and rest, while jetties run off at an angle to provide platforms over the water

Opposite, above right: Detail of bench with integrated light

Above: The individual jetties over the water enforce a connection between the water and the waterside walkways

Below: At night the entrances to the park are celebrated by lighted beacons, right, while areas under the trees, left, provide sanctuary for private get-togethers

Parkland

Fontsanta Park
Barcelona, Spain, 2001
Manuel Ruisánchez

Above: Cross-section of the site along the former riverbed

Below: General site landscape plan. The defunct river course is emphasized by its conversion to a central pathway

Over the past decade the proportion of schemes that might be defined as 'landscape recovery' projects has been larger than ever before. The category is distinct from that of pure landscape conservation, and the typology has been largely ignored by conservationists. The landscapes that fall into the 'recovery' category reflect man's abuse of his environment. Where economy and expediency rule, environmental eyesores are created. They are usually either chemically or physically dangerous to local inhabitants, and sometimes both. Abandoned military zones also fall into this category, whether used for weapons testing or exercises, or as battlefields, airfields or minefields. Large areas of rural Afghanistan, following high-technology precision bombing, are one such example, as were the trenches of the Somme after the First World War. The more general detritus of industrial and commercial development represents another category. (See Emscher Park by Peter Latz, pp.38–45)

This landscape phenomenon has been artificially created and is truly global in extent. Only in the twenty-first century is society beginning, spasmodically, to address the problem. Progress is still marginal, against the proliferation of new sites of blight and decay, the dumps for lethal waste and abandoned consumer products. The landscape architect's method is more akin here to that of the archaeologist or geologist in plotting the extent and condition of waste material, and its massive impact on the previously existing landscape. Then comes the process of reinventing the location, taking all historical impacting into consideration before establishing a new template for ecological and human engagement.

Fontsanta Park on the outskirts of Barcelona is the result of a competition organized by the city's civic authorities in 1994. The winner was the Spanish landscape architect Manuel Ruisánchez. In 2000 work was completed, and today the gradual, natural rehabilitation of the landscape can be seen taking full effect.

The Fontsanta scheme serves as a useful metaphor. It represents the combination of a realistic, natural rehabilitation process with an economically viable policy. The project recognizes the consolidation of impacted urban waste deposits, without necessitating their costly removal. This is no restoration or conservation exercise.

When true parkland is to be designed, the presence of water in some form is invariably a bonus. By the same token, a site that was formed by a pre-existing river seems to demand that it be reinstated. At Fontsanta, the existing drainage regime seemed to make this wholly impractical. Infrastructural and microclimatic changes had resulted from the drying-up of the river. Only a trace of its original course could be seen below the serrated, corrugated profile of

blocks of waste, dumped there over previous decades. Despite the pre-existing geology and topography, a wholly new pattern of irregular wedges and gullies had recast the contours of the old river edge to create one long ravine. It is in the nature of ravines, as with quarry sites, to cause remarkable extremes of temperature. Ruisánchez and his team exploited this in their choice of planting for the area, introducing species of gorse, elm and mimosa to flourish in the gullies, accompanied by willows, tamarinds and olives to harmonize with the vegetation which had already taken root during the period of dumping and dereliction.

In its heyday the dump had operated as a buffer between an industrial zone and a housing area, a fact that had seemed utterly irrelevant to the authorities that sanctioned it. A more enlightened civic authority in the closing decade of the twentieth century realized that a landscaped park on the same site would provide an area for walking, playing and rambling, enhancing and even bringing together the neighbouring areas of residential and industrial land. Office and industrial workers needed somewhere to take their breaks and to relax in all seasons, while local inhabitants were also short of parks.

Through a process of accurately plotting the topography and topology of the waste tips, creating new, man-made terraces of strong, gabion construction and then stabilizing them with topsoil, the avalanching rubbish debris has been replaced by a profusion of planting that now cascades down the same slopes, accumulating naturally at the bottom of the gullies. The newly-planted areas of ash and maple establish rapidly, and ample groves have developed in Elysian profusion. On the embankment stretches of the old river, robinia and vine plantations create a perfect contrast. Spring flowers now proliferate where empty cans and broken bottles once blocked life.

The tumbling ravines occur two dozen or so times, in varying form, all reaching the river bed at the bottom of a 30-metre (100 foot) descent. Tantalizingly, like a spring source, a pond is established at the head of the river valley. The brilliant stroke in the Ruisánchez plan is to emphasize the absence of this river, to capitalize on the reality of the location's history. He provides a continuous zigzagging pathway which runs along the original riverbed. This is punctuated occasionally by terracing or shaded resting points, and runs through more open, meadow-like swathes of grass. Literally, Ruisánchez has taken a line for a walk.

At the climax or 'estuary' of the river line, there is a contoured open area which now contains a football pitch, with a gradual ascent to the car-parking area. Fontsanta Park is already a success, with the contrasting activities, the cheering and playing, at one end and the small

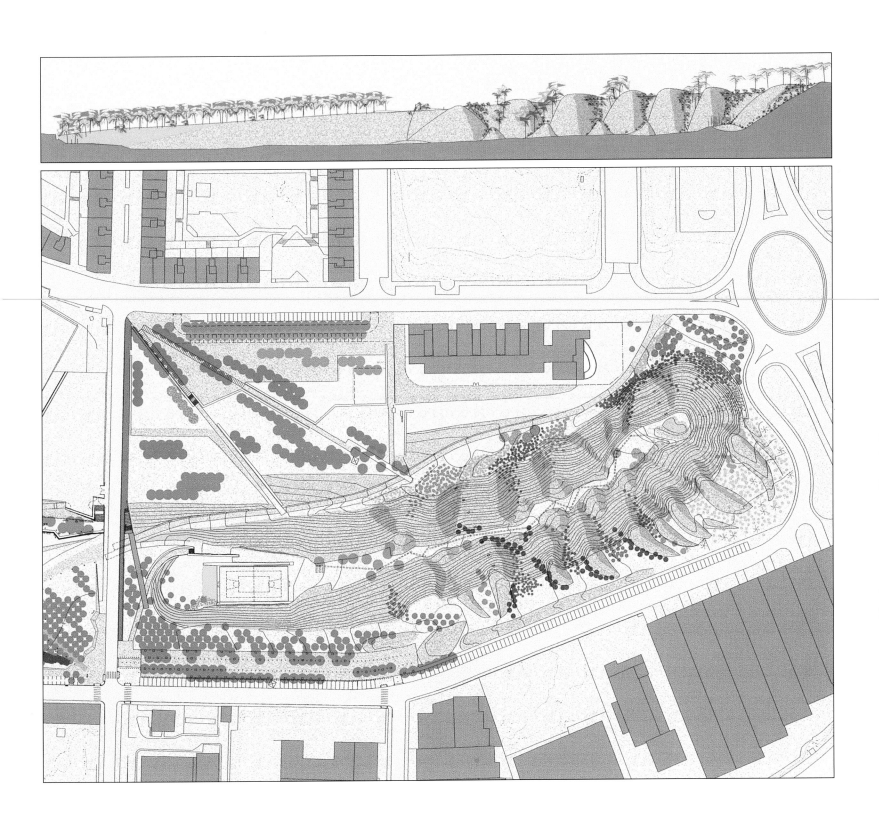

Fontsanta Park

Right: View down the valley along the old river course, now converted into a landscaped path

Above: From the entrance to the park, continuous terracing marks the pedestrian walkways down into the park, overlooking the areas of green sanctuary below

Below: Pedestrian access is separated from the vehicular route to the edge of the site

contemplative lake at the upper end of the river line. It seems it will always now be in use, a valuable, re-oxygenated 'lung' for all those who live and work nearby. For this reason Fontsanta Park is more than an outstanding Catalonian solution to a local eyesore. It can be seen as a working example for the necessary transformations, *sans frontières*, which contemporary landscape designers must increasingly achieve in the face of the massive and accumulating legacy of dereliction of our time. This simple, definitive project both epitomizes society's urgent dilemma and symbolizes the way out of the problem.

Parkland

West Point Wastewater Treatment Plant, Seattle, USA, 1999

Danadjieva & Koenig Associates

The Magnolia neighbourhood of Seattle is perhaps the most select in the city. Its residents enjoy a remarkable degree of privacy on account of the military base close to West Point, only decommissioned in the 1980s. This closure brought new planning issues into play. The existing sewage treatment plant was earmarked for a massive expansion, as the protective ring of military buildings around the installation had suddenly vanished. It was as if the Emperor had no clothes, or that was the general feeling of the residents of Magnolia whose houses overlooked the Puget Sound. A new 216-hectare (535-acre) park, to be known as Discovery Park, was planned for the former military site. The influential householders of Magnolia now found their equity profoundly endangered by the planned extension of the West Point sewage plant. The scene was set for a major confrontation. At this point the city of Seattle had the intelligence and foresight to commission landscape architects Danadjieva and Koenig Associates to make plans that would render the essential expansion of the plant less than visible.

Angela Danadjieva trained at the École des Beaux Arts in Paris. Born in Bulgaria, she had worked there as a set designer and model-maker in the national film industry. After training, she gained experience in the Lawrence Halprin Partnership of San Francisco. This varied experience gave her the confidence to accept the challenge from the Seattle authorities, who already knew her work with Halprin on Freeway Park in the city. In that project, a downtown area split by the construction of Interstate Route 5 had been reconciled using various water elements and dramatic plantings across a huge decking.

Danadjieva had learnt much from Halprin. For West Point, where $578 million dollars'-worth of sewage treatment works was to be hidden without trace by landscaping, Danadjieva negotiated a special budget of $86.7 million as a 'mitigation' fund. One possible solution, considered but soon eliminated by Danadjieva, was to enclose the whole plant within a massive landscaped 'lid'. She wisely surmised that landscape design might offer other, more ingenious ways of resolving the issue.

Danadjieva and Koenig Associates realized that the solution was to work with the actual site contours of West Point, reducing the optimal area of the treatment works. A 'footprint' of 32 hectares (80 acres) was posited by the engineers, but this was replaced by an actual site area of only 12 hectares (30 acres). With more careful landscape planning the entire plant could be 'shoehorned' into the smaller area. Around this reserved area the designers created a 1000-metre (3,500-foot) retaining wall, rising as high as 18 metres (60 feet) in places and incorporating 27,000 cubic metres (35,000 cubic yards) of composted soil, in which extensive planting was embedded. From the early stages, Danadjieva used a series of contoured models to evolve the optimal arrangement for undulating concrete walls among which the public could actually walk, past deep-planted trees and shrubs. The formal, sculptural definition of this element was fine-tuned by computer-generated wire-frame drawings. From these, Danadjieva evolved highly atmospheric sketches, demonstrating the wealth of natural wilderness planting through which public paths would wind. Later, she was to position the various trees and plants personally, to maximize ground cover, and views for the walkers. It was not necessary to roof over the entire site since, as Danadjieva proved, there were very few points from which the plant became visible on-site. Instead, the architectural solution of constructing the undulating, sculpted concrete walls provided a new topology, designed both to conceal the outline of the plant and to guide the walker through a contoured landscape garden. Some 13,000 trees, 51,500 shrubs and 133,000 ground-cover plants were imported to the site, together with 100,000 'plugs' of beach grasses. Speed and consistency of growth is ensured by a far-reaching irrigation system.

The chronology of this massive project is thought-provoking, and also demonstrates how public and civic attitudes have changed over half a century. In 1952, on the superb landmark site of West Point, the city was able to establish the initial $12.9 million sewage treatment plant with little public protest. It was dedicated some ten years later with much civic pride. At that time the 12-hectare (30-acre) site was granted to the military. In 1972 Fort Lawton was handed over to the city authorities, to become the lushly afforested and planted Discovery Park. So visible had the old sewage plant by then become that in 1987, Seattle's Mayor Royer identified an obvious vote-winner by establishing a feasibility plan for demolition and removal of the plant. It now transpired, however, that the water currents around West Point were perfect for the outfall of treated water and its dispersal. And so it came to be in our more environmentally conscious age that ingenuity prevailed over pure expediency.

In the final analysis one can recognize at West Point a special commitment to spatial sculptural design in landscape projects that is a West Coast triumph. While the influence of

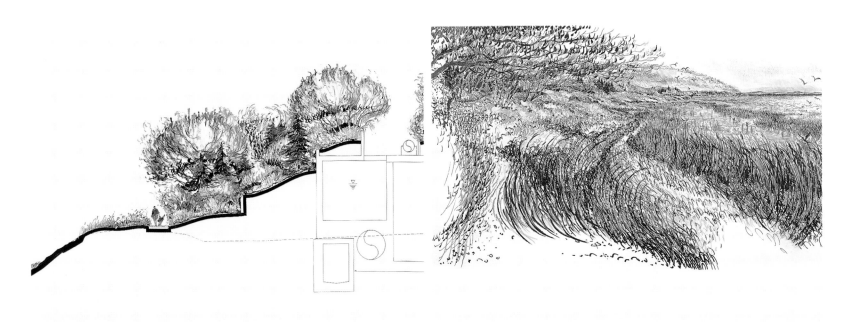

Right: Construction of the retaining walls

Far right: Contour-based conformation of the walls, concealing the water treatment units

Opposite, above left and right: natural vegetation again proliferates, supplemented by carefully selected species

Opposite, below: Access road users remain oblivious to the mass of the treatment plant concealed throughout

Halprin's approach to topology, contour and vista is instrumental in Danadjieva and Koenig Associates' superlative resolution of the manifold dilemmas of West Point, it is clear that Angela Dandjieva's meticulous modelling of the options for this site, coupled with her hands-on approach to the distribution of a massive planting programme within a remarkably tight budget, has brought the overall scheme to complete success. This would not have been possible, however, without civic vision, intelligent costing and remarkable courage of conviction and commitment on the part of the landscape architects, whose co-ordinating role was also critical. The parklands that have been created for access by both the inhabitants of Magnolia and the citizens of Seattle represent a massive

environmental dividend, as well as an ingenious solution (that has ultimately benefited the public purse) over all other theoretical design and planning options available. Danadjieva and Koenig Associates have, in other words, presided over a triumph for visionary landscape design as well as for civic expediency.

Parkland

**Yuma East Wetlands
Colorado River, USA, 2002**

Fred Phillips

This major landscape project acknowledged a respected line of practical precedent emanating from both the east and the west of the United States. The initial re-orientation of landscape design towards resources planning was fostered by Ian McHarg at the University of Pennsylvania. His revolutionary reappraisal of priorities was published in 1964.[1] In extending the basis of landscape architecture McHarg became a major catalyst, increasing public awareness, not only in America but also in Europe, of the environmental and indeed ethical basis for the profession. Latterly, Kenneth Frampton has persistently argued for more collective, ecological patterns of land settlement; seeing the 'blanket application of landscape interventions, in one form or another, as a way of improving the environmental harshness of large tracts of our urbanized regions.'[2] He has also argued at length for the revegetation of land and for new tree planting to be applied for ecological reasons, as a coordinated public programme, including planted berms. Frampton's primary concern was, of course, a strategy for the urban regional ecology. But the idea of landscape as a redemptive strategy has broader implications, whereby all societies, more or less developed, address the total landscape as a precious and diminishing resource.

The teaching of landscape architect John Lyle (1934–98), transmitted through his important publication *Regenerative Design for Sustainable Development*,[3] has taken the resources-based argument further, urging the nation as a whole to focus on the depletion of natural resources and landscapes as a result of widespread and uncontrolled industrial processes. Throughout his career, Lyle observed the continual degradation of natural resources and the landscapes which contain them. Latterly, Andropogon Associates, with whom Lyle worked before his early death, developed Crosby Arboretum in the Picayune locality of the Gulf South across a network of 688 hectares (1,700 acres) in three Southern Mississippi counties, saving native plant habitats as a genetic archive.

The work of landscape architect Fred Phillips falls naturally within this succession, through his seven years' research and development for the Yuma East Wetlands project within the massive lower Colorado River area. Dams, new agriculture and the introduction of certain exotic plant species seemed to have drastically altered the wetlands ecosystem, replacing indigenous trees such as mesquite bosques and cottonwood or willow gallery forests. The backwaters, beaches and forests around, long cherished for

hunting, recreation and education, were diminished and deteriorating fast.

Phillips' plan was executed with some urgency, despite the fact that his most useful form of transport was his own canoe. His scheme was accomplished by means of natural channel design: water flow was restored in these degraded wetlands, and aquatic habitats and various schemes for the revegetation of banks were developed. The statistics make interesting reading: there are 445 hectares (1,100 acres) of riparian habitat, 60 hectares (148 acres) of open water, 40 hectares (98 acres) of marshland and, perhaps symbolically, 8 hectares (20 acres) of agricultural land. As a whole, the area accommodates over 300 species of birds, 32 species of mammals, 19 species of fish, 20 species of reptiles and 9 amphibian species. It was hardly a desert, and these characteristics demonstrate only the urgency of habitat design, protection and proper enhancement to prevent further extinction, so encouraging in due course renewed movement of migratory birds. A revegetation plan by Phillips envisaged planting over 300,000 indigenous trees over an initial 100-hectare (250-acre) tract.

Lucy Lippard, in *The Lure of the Local*,[4] drew attention to the inherent paradox of the conflict of modernity with the native Colorado tribes, where the Arapaho were found trying to expel invasive rituals and to remove so-called 'offerings'. In the words of an Arapaho elder, 'there was no need to change what was physically present because the power is still there and the site needed no cosmetic improvements.' And this site was actually within the Boulder city limits. Such philosophy was understood by Fred Phillips at Yuma, as he set about enhancing water courses by dredging and excavating natural channels. The revegetation plan itself will recover native stands of trees. The necessary re-introduction of seasonal flooding will eventually end the damming and confinement of rivers, and so bring back the natural process of soil desalination. Phillips engaged the support of the Quechon native tribe, and Dennis Patch, a member of the Colorado River Indian Tribes Council. Patch had himself sought ways of preserving the landscape of woodlands and wetlands which he had known as a child, before the changing priorities of farmers and home-owners changed the flow of the Colorado River, which had historically been highly sedimented.

At Purdue University, Indiana, Bernie Dahl, assistant professor to Kent Schuette on the landscape architectural programme, had early in his career rescued an uninspired

Opposite, left: Sunset over
Yuma East Wetlands

Opposite, right, and this page:
Banks of the Colorado river,
revegetated with native plants
and trees to encourage
marshland bird and animal
species

Phillips and introduced him to a non-traditional,
environmentally-based approach to landscape. In due
course, working with Patch, Phillips inspired the Bureau of
Indian Affairs to make an initial grant of $10,000 to fund tree-
planting over a trial area of 0.8 hectares (2 acres). Then,
during 1995 and 1996, up to nine Purdue students were
recruited in stages. Soon, working with the general support
of the whole community, native Indians included, Phillips
secured over $5 million in tribal, state and federal grants to
support the project for the restoration of wetland and riparian
woodland, establishing also a native plant nursery, a nature
park and an environmental education project for tribal
members and visitors alike. By the year 2000, over 340
hectares (850 acres) had already been restored.

Phillips and the project foreman Victor Cuadrashave
worked with the Navajos, Hopi, Chemehueri and Mojave
tribes who inhabit this 108,502-hectare (268,000-acre)
reservation. As tribal elder and shaman John Scott says of
Phillips, 'what he has done is a beautiful thing.' Phillips, in
return, likes to quote Scott: 'Once you touch something you
need to care for it. We have touched almost the entire planet,
and now we need to take care of it.' This can be said to be a
particularly effective vindication of the pastoral, positive,

caring mode which contemporary theorists today propagate
in the concerns of landscape designers for a better world.[5] It
seems all the more appropriate to include this project in a
selection of case studies which as a rule focus on the more
immediate preoccupations of urbanized man.

1 Ian McHarg, *Design with Nature*, New York/Chichester: John Wiley &
Sons, Inc, 1992. Originally published Garden City, NY: Published for the
American Museum of Natural History by the Natural History Press, 1964
2 Kenneth Frampton, 'Seven Points for the Millennium', *Architectural
Review*, London, Nov 1999, p.78. This is an edited version of Frampton's paper
to the UIA Conference, Beijing, August 1999
3 John Lyle, *Regenerative Design for Sustainable Development*, New
York/Chichester: John Wiley & Sons, Inc, 1993
4 Lucy Lippard, *The Lure of the Local: The Sense of Place in a Multicentred
Society*, The New Press, 1997
5 Tom Campbell, 'Grad makes trees grow and waters flow: Arizona
internship blossoms into 6-year project', in *Purdue Agriculture Connections*,
Purdue University, (AGAD, West Lafayette, Indiana, USA) vol 10, no 1, Winter
2001, p 3

**Barcelona Botanic Gardens
Barcelona, Spain, 2000**

Bet Figueras

The site for the new botanic garden of Barcelona was very carefully chosen, high above the city itself, with a view across the delta of the Llobregat river. Examples of modern botanic gardens are unusual. Barcelona's 15-hectare (37-acre) site on the south-western slope of Montjuic is perfectly positioned for a garden which sets out to provide no less than a narrative of the natural Mediterranean landscape. Bet Figueras won the commission in 1997 as the result of an international competition. Her previous experience in practice was predominantly in the design of relatively small domestic gardens. Viewing her profession as a craft, she pursues the development of a scheme through initial focus on the planting requirements, choosing plants appropriate to the site and the micro-climate. The same principles have been applied here on a larger scale. In some of her earlier gardens, Figueras used elements of abstract geometry, extending and harmonizing with the inherent structural format of the immediate buildings. She has always made use of the movement and energy of water wherever possible. This is particularly evident in such garden projects as the Jardí al Carrer Abadessa d'Olzet and the Terrassa a Sarrià, both in Barcelona.

Here on the Montjuic slope Figueras has imposed a carefully formulated narrative about the evolution of the Mediterranean landscape, laying it out in such a way that the landscape plan forms the basis for long-term propagation and husbandry of the selected plants. To achieve this, as her plan shows, she has derived a delicate latticework of paths from the indigenously wooded summit of the park, adapting to the natural contours but establishing a loosely triangulated grid. This enables the organizational aspects of taxonomy and widely varying seasonal growth patterns of plants to be accounted for, and allows development to proceed readily over a long-term cycle of change. What has been referred to by critics as a kind of fractal landscape is echoed in the overtly tectonic entry pavilions and enclosures. Where contour necessitates deep folds in the landscape she has employed cutting and filling techniques to hold back compacted earthworks, retaining these earth walls with Cor-Ten steel wedges.

As the site layout plan indicates, entry to the Botanic Gardens is to the north-west side of the hill. After passing through the normal reception process, the visitor can follow a chronological sequence of development, from indigenous woodland and scrub at the south-eastern boundary, moving gradually and steadily northwards. This is important in terms of the heat in summer, when the majority of visitors will come. At the upper section of the site, close to the northern edge, more intensively grown species are organized in five rectilinear sections, with plants laid out in rows for more efficient cultivation and watering. Figueras uses such elements as wooden planks, triangulated areas of harder landscaping, and of course water and waterside planting to moderate the more natural, indigenous sections. The loose and flexible mesh of paths will allow planting to proceed on a pragmatic basis, since one can never exactly foretell the effects of microclimate, when no deliberate planting or horticulture has previously occupied a virgin soil. In other words, the twenty-first century botanical landscape carries its own inherent degree of experimentation, appropriate for a post-Darwinian age.

Unlike the Eden project conceived by Tim Smit with Nicholas Grimshaw, the Montjuic project is open to the elements. This allows for the creation of varying micro-climatic effects. In many respects Figueras' design is the product of a twenty-first century vision. Sir Geoffrey Jellicoe (1900–96) displayed a similarly visionary sense when, in 1984, he proposed a unique botanic garden for a 50-hectare (123-acre) site on wetlands at the northern edge of the island city of Galveston, Texas, on the inhospitable Gulf of Mexico. Similarly, his Moody Botanical Gardens, Galveston Island, Texas were laid out in a highly organized gridwork of plant areas. These were linked by waterways along which visitors could also be conveyed in flat barges through a combination of untamed landscape (the wetlands) and scientifically organized botanical display. The narrative at Moody was that of botanical evolution, no less, laid out in a pattern of rhythmic spaces with the same cohesion and underlying harmony as a musical score. Figueras' method of guiding the hillside visitor by means of a cohesive structure of paths through a scientific narrative is equally challenging. Montjuic does not permit as many as 50 spaces, and many may remain under-utilized or immature for some considerable time. The effect, however, is not dissimilar. In Figueras' botanic garden, Mediterranean species can flourish in an organized manner, and certain mental images of Mediterranean landscape can be recreated. She focuses in particular on the cultivated, terraced landscape of growing plants, linked by walkways or goat tracks. Figueras says that 'as the spatial order was to take botanical requirements into due consideration, the articulation of the gardens was to be largely determined by the distribution of plants, and given

a basic geometric structure at the same time.'[6] The plants also provide her with a palette of colours. 72 plant 'communities' have been composed, spanning the ecology from water-based species, through all varieties of soil, to the indigenous mountain forest itself. Within the gardens innumerable overlaps and cross-propagations occur comfortably within the flexible geometry of planned propagation areas.

Figueras' so-called 'fractal' landscape thus represents a formal abstraction of the great wealth of Mediterranean land husbandry in all its traditional patterns. The detailing of the wide joints between the concrete surfaces of the paths harmonizes the various deliberate angularities on an irregular, site-specific basis. The steeper slopes have

reinforced layers of earth, and steel mats are even utilized to retain soil. The Cor-Ten steel walls seem to blend naturally into this postmodern symphony, with the colours and the soil itself. This is an educational garden of discovery. The visitor must abandon all preconceptions about the traditional botanical urban garden. He or she may now wander along the terraces, secure in the topology that even a child can subconsciously master.

6 *Topos*, 29, 1999

Barcelona Botanic Gardens

Above and centre: Focal point for maintenance storage, a massive circular area

Below: General landscape plan of the Botanic Garden, with its network of public access paths

Opposite: Figueras' careful incorporation of 'fractal' rhythmic spaces, angular pathways, seating and water features

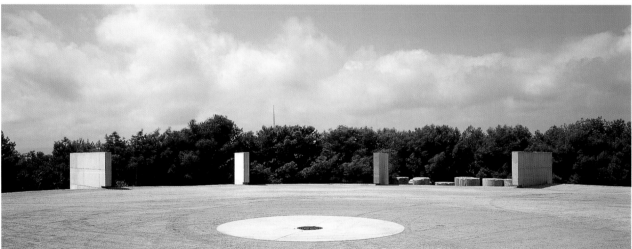

Architecture as Landscape

Current architectural developments that fall into the category of 'buildings in the landscape' draw upon an array of precedents, a long-established body of ideas. There is, however, a major difference between that and the concept of 'Architecture as Landscape'. To a considerable extent this metaphorical paradigm, evident in isolated projects since the nineteenth century, was legitimized by a growing awareness of the fragility of the landscape within which new buildings are sited. This awareness has been invoked and stimulated by the work of Land Artists and Installation Artists, through their commitment to the surface of the Earth. It was no surprise that such perceptions emerged in the United States, through the work of the Californians Michael Heizer and Walter de Maria. The long history of the American Sublime, and its recognition of the inpenetrability of the wild through landscape painting, provided a clear precedent for a return to the real as epitomized by such work. In this expanded field, as Hal Foster has elaborated, 'Minimalism appears as a historical crux in which the formalist autonomy of art is at once achieved and broken up.'[1] Initially explored by Robert Smithson, this process then opened the way for landscape designers. The most articulate on the subject has undoubtedly been Peter Walker.

More recently, a quite different genre of artists has emerged in Europe. Their work epitomizes growing human concern over the diminishing natural resources of the planet. Artists such as Richard Long, Hamish Fulton, Giuseppe Penone and Chris Drury apply differing modes of perception, collection and manipulation of natural materials. It is indeed this concern with the material world that sets them further apart from their American colleagues. Yet it can be said without reserve that their impact upon the perception of architects and landscape designers is pervasive; and as Peter Walker has realized, it is through the philosophy of Minimalism that such work generates acts of collusion by such designers. The lesser-known paintings of Niklaus Lang and the English artist David Blackburne reflect the same reverence for fragments of nature. Lang's work in turn has been inspired by Aboriginal interaction with the desert in Australia.

It is clear that American and European parameters overlap, although no circle will ever be closed. The combined effect of such work produces a new momentum of open vision, making redundant both the idea of 'the academy' and also that of an 'avant-garde'.

It was never predicated as a basic principle of building that the built form should be subsumed by the surrounding site. Invariably architecture, whether vernacular or monumental, has stood clear of its natural or gardened surround, which itself is then dedicated to the architecture and its aspirations. Such buildings may conform to the existing contours and topography; indeed these can in turn formulate a new topology, incorporating the needs of car-parking or sunken shopping malls. Examples of such schemes are illustrated in the main introduction. Materials of construction have always played a key role, and climatic, geological and

Richard Long, Mountain Lake, Powder Snow, Lapland (1985)

Niklaus Lang, *Brainship* (1987–90), cotton paper pulp, gauze, bamboo spruce sticks. (Flinders' Range, Australia)

social criteria have provided for local or regional variations which become apparent in the built scheme.

Elsewhere, the concept of an architecture 'in denial' has evolved. Niklaus Pevsner's famous claim that a bicycle shed is a building while Lincoln Cathedral is a piece of architecture has long been abandoned.[2] Such major surveys as Paul Oliver's *Encyclopaedia of Vernacular Architecture of the World* have revealed the richness and sophistication of different types of buildings, and transformed the very meaning of the word 'architecture'. Today, the elegance of design and build in natural materials is exemplified in Edward Cullinan's gridshell museum workshop (Weald and Downland Museum, 2002). The vernacular idiom emerged via computer-aided design, utilizing local oak. The computer is the new hand-tool of the global vernacular. As this built shell slips elegantly into the embrace of the woodland, it is a celebration of 'architecture as landscape', in the hands of a pastoral practitioner and architect of a new definition as urged by Kenneth Frampton.

Frampton has single-handedly led a revision theory through his re-presentation of tectonic principles in architecture.[3] Architectural theories in the nineteenth century posited a primordial dwelling, divided into four basic elements: 1) the earthwork, 2) the hearth, 3) the framework/roof and 4) the lightweight enclosing membrane. This standpoint enabled the German theorist Gottfried Semper to break down building systems of the time still further.[4] In his analysis, attention was drawn to: a) the tectonics of the frame and b) the 'stereotomics' of the earthwork.[5] Hitherto, it had been assumed that the latter always relied upon loadbearing masonry. Today, where lightness and heaviness in structure have taken on different meanings, these help to define the architecture that can 'sit lightly' on the landscape, as distinct from such buildings as are avowedly embedded in the soil or diffused within it.

There is more to consider, however, than the elementary factors of lightness and mass: the definition of any place exercises a formative role *per se*. Alvar Aalto was one of the very first Modernists to believe in analysing the existing site topology before extending this search into the paths, routes and interstitial spaces, which all then return to celebrate the building's primary functional spaces, whether auditoria, libraries, galleries or concert halls. In the free hierarchies of Aalto we are reminded of the paths, openings and clearings in the forest.[6]

By salutary contrast, one might look at a particular landscape-defined project of great significance to its community: the Scottish Parliament by Enric Miralles and Benedetta Tagliabue. The architects' competition-winning scheme dramatically extended a formal unity with the ancient volcanic landscape, and deliberate efforts were made to formulate by allusion and metaphor a localized apparatus of tectonic significance, reminiscent of salient, generalized features of the landscape. These references included upended fishing boats expressive, Miralles thought, of a Scottish identity.

Edward Cullinan Architects, Archaeolink Prehistoric Centre, Aberdeenshire (2001). This project for an on-site visitor's centre by Cullinan embeds the building in earthworks, effectively simulating prehistoric built form

Miralles commendably sought to build a Parliament that will be 'not in Edinburgh but in the land of Scotland'. The contradiction, given the essentially urban siting, suggests a dialectical framework; but arguably a uniquely stereotomic solution or even a predominantly urban manifestation was a prerequisite. It was not to be architecture as landscape by this definition, whatever else has emerged.

In Miralles' and Pinõs' design for the Igualada Cemetery (1991) in Catalonia, the architecture by contrast is drawn deep down into the earth by natural topographical recesses. The parameters for an architecture that aspires to enhance landscape, rather than dominate it, are finely drawn and are exceeded only at peril. Every scheme must be founded anew.

In Portugal, a new precedent emerged when Leslie Martin created the Gallery of Contemporary Art, Gulbenkian Foundation, Lisbon (1979–83). It had no propensity either to accommodate significant allusion or invoke metaphor. Martin chose to celebrate the juxtaposition of the parkland site and the lake in front of it. The design incorporated stepped-back galleries, creating two roof areas that offered space for a substantial amount of planting.

A more recent building in Portugal, the Moledo House (1998) by Eduardo Souta de Moura, sets up a series of vernacular drystone terraces along the site contours, looking out over the Atlantic with all the stereotomic implication of an ancient, yet neatly trimmed, vineyard. While these walls are a century old, they also have a Minimalist quality inherent to their original role. At the rear of the house, site topography is again respected. The glass wall runs adjacent to the sheer site rock itself, a magical proximity of separation that reminds one of the precedent of Glasgow's Burrell Museum (1972–83) by Barry Gasson, Brit Andresen and John Meunier, there found between gallery and woodland precinct.

The imperative for an architecture embracing the Earth frequently assumes a definitive regional connotation: the Museum of Vulcanology by Hans Hollein, for example, reduces the disturbance of the exposed volcanic site to an absolute minimum, while still incorporating a dramatic, truncated cone. Typically for Hollein, this scheme was presented as both autochthonic (literally 'sprung from the Earth') and indigenous. Hollein's earlier Salzburg Guggenheim Art Museum project (1986) exploited an escarpment rising opposite the city. Here he excavated within the rock a feature known as the *Sunk*; thus the entire museum is made below ground. It is not tectonic, but simply atectonic, bringing with it the opportunity of carving space so relished by this architect.[7]

At the other extreme, Daniel Libeskind's Imperial War Museum North, Manchester is seen to have established its own building topography. It rises, through geological allusions to land movement, to an 'air shard' from which a promontory is created overlooking the prevailing flat industrial and commercial landscape, and the ship canal below. The architect had created his own landscape to such an extent that when unfortunate budgetary

Leslie Martin, Gulbenkian Foundation, Gallery of Contemporary Art, Lisbon, Portugal (1979–83)

reductions removed the landscape proposed by Charles Jencks, the loss was effectively concealed.

Harmonious landscape collusion of a different kind is evident in two other case studies in this section. The first, the European Film College, Ebeltoft by Heikkinen and Komonen, reveals a subtle but total affiliation with land form. The buildings are disposed along the surface contours like alluvial-driven boulders in a glacier. In Australia, Glenn Murcutt's Arthur and Yvonne Boyd Education Centre runs gently along the incline, the falling ground providing space for a further level of accommodation.

In an interesting small-scale accommodation of house with landscape surround, Colin St John Wilson and M J Long in the Cornford House, Spring Road, Cambridge (1967) opened the essentially 'stereotomic' volume outwards to embrace the surrounding trees, on a diagonal axis, which movement was accentuated by the articulation of timber columns, beams, struts and ties fully exposed. The terrace created, a form of two-storey verandah, provides the definitive inside/outside space: it epitomizes the transition and enhances both aspects.[8]

The contemporary tendency to affiliate architecture and landscape wherever possible has emerged, as we have seen, against a powerfully evolved materialization of two strands of artistic endeavour, Land Art and Art in Nature. As Minimalist art has also decreed, the finest of lines separates perfection, balanced between order and chaos, from mere parody and banality. Landscape designers and architects accordingly bring their skills together in this, perhaps the hardest of tasks, and one that requires the greatest sacrifice of previously-held conventions.

Notes

1 Hal Foster, *The Return of the Real*, Cambridge, MA: MIT Press, 1996, ch 2, 'The Crux of Minimalism', p.36

2 Niklaus Pevsner, *An Outline of European Architecture*, Jubilee Edition, London: Allen Lane, 1973, p.7

3 For the best definition of stereotomic and tectonic, see Stanford Anderson, 'Modern Architecture and Industry: Peter Behrens, the AEG and Industrial Design', *Oppositions*, 21, Cambridge, MA: MIT Press, Summer 1980. Tectonic referred (in *Die Tektonik der Hellenen* by Karl Bottischer) not just to the activity 'of making the materially requisite construction … but rather to the activity that raises this construction to an art form … The functionally adequate form must be adapted so as to give expression to its function.'

4 See Gottfried Semper, *Die vier Elemente der Baukunst* (1851), trans. as *Four Elements of Architecture and Other Writings* by F Mallgrave and W Herman, Cambridge: Cambridge University Press, 1989. Sourced in commentary by Kenneth Frampton in *Studies in Tectonic Culture* (ed. J Cava), Cambridge, MA: MIT Press, 1995, p.5

5 The 'stereotomics' in building are the compressive mass of the same, as opposed to the 'tectonics' of the building frame itself

6 For a full exposition of this aspect of Aalto's topological approach, see Michael Spens, 'New York Before and After', *Architectural Design*, vol. 68, no. 11/12, Nov/Dec 1998, pp.*vi–x*. Also lecture by Aalto, Swedish Craft Centre, Stockholm (Swedish Society of Industrial Design, 9 May 1935)

7 'Atectonic' is literally a building form without tectonic qualities. Hans Hollein's Salzburg Guggenheim Art Museum (1986) exemplifies this condition, being sunk into the site, hence avoiding disruption of the historic, city centre view. See Michael Spens, 'Sunk in the Berg: Museum Project by Hans Hollein', *Architectural Review*, Jan 1992

8 This house typifies a clear tectonic differentiation between the stereotomic mass of the house and its tectonic open roof structure which embraces the garden surround, opening to reveal the inner poetics of the central space, at the same time revealing columns, struts and ties in a highly articulated form of two-level veranda. See Michael Spens, 'The Presence of Absence: The Cambridge House for Christopher Cornford by Colin St John Wilson', *Architectural Research Quarterly*, Oct 1996

Architecture as Landscape

Imperial War Museum North
Salford, Manchester, UK, 2002
Studio Libeskind

There is a longstanding precedent of important institutional or religious buildings being located in prominent waterside locations. Usually a landscape element coincides with the architectural topology within such a landscape, engendering a process of dramatic transformation. It is not necessary to recall Palladio's church to the Redentore (the Redeemer, 1577) in the flat lagoon of Venice, or even San Giorgio Maggiore itself, even though these are relevant as precedents. Frank Gehry's Guggenheim Museum in Bilbao with its vertical, horizontal and waterside elements demonstrated, albeit with a conventional enough plan, such a distinctive ordering of priorities. In this context it is impossible to ignore the superlative qualities of Daniel Libeskind's Imperial War Museum North, set beside the Manchester ship canal. The museum literally reaches for the sky in a most memorable way, and the Lowry building opposite benignly provides the foil, a contrasting secular heaviness such as that of the Arsenale viewed across the Grand Canal from the soaring San Giorgio Maggiore in Venice. In Manchester too, the conjunction of light and space works well.

The building was fittingly described by Arup, its engineer, as comprising 'a scaled-down representation of the Earth. On a macro-scale there is chaos, but on a micro-scale the Earth has many systems of perfect order working next to each other. The structural system for the building is exactly the same.' Libeskind even created a new, gently curved first-floor surface for the gallery in order to avoid and separate the contaminated site datum.

The museum is a memory container, a cephalic node where the mnemonic essence of war is laid on dramatically, rather than liturgically infused as in a religious shrine. Some 15.5 million inhabitants now live within two hours of this contemporary landmark: a fair proportion still recall the wartime blitzing of the Old Trafford area of Salford where the Museum is sited. Libeskind here opens up the landscape of the in-between, between rigid totalities and chaotic histories of conflict.

It is a curious coincidence that this building establishes itself by means of a cavernous interior similar to that of the Vulcanology Museum by Hans Hollein (see pp.94–9), opened in the same year; cavernous that is, internally, where the topology is absolutely predicated by the external morphology of site and surrounds. Libeskind recognizes that in landscape, disorientation and route-finding go together. The architectural presumption of predictable signs for navigation is not followed here, as it has been in the Guggenheim Bilbao, for example. Instead, manoeuvring around the Museum, both inside and out, becomes essentially a landscape experience, with all the uncertainties and bonuses of a natural construct.

The surrounding area had some of the post-war desolation also apparent in the location of Libeskind's new Jewish Museum in Berlin. But in Manchester, it is the silver filament of the ship canal which provides the topological focus. With great resourcefulness, Libeskind achieved a miracle of economy and architectural professionalism within a budget of £28.5 million. He drastically revised the materials schedule and, by postponing construction of the auditorium (still planned) and converting the structure to steel and aluminium cladding, maintained virtually unchanged the dramatic formal composition with which he had won the competition, despite the abandonment of concrete. But an ironic and unwarranted loss was the external landscaping and planting. Familiarity with the diversity and allegorical richness of the landscaping designed by Libeskind and others around the Jewish Museum in Berlin can only underline the loss. And yet what transpires from this further economy is the reality that such additions are not missed – Libeskind's building creates its own unique and moving landscape, shimmering by the wharf. The building rises with the hard-textured, unadorned profile of a small volcano, the fragmented 'shards' clad with aluminium, gleaming in the frequent rainfall or glowing in the sun. It is the bland tree plantations around the more recent neighbouring business parks which appear artificial, almost synthetic, in their separation from natural form.

The underlying concept for the Imperial War Museum derived in gesture from the pieces of a fragmented globe. Leaving three major shards lying, Libeskind realized how these pieces seemed to contain the poetry and the pathos of war. He chose to interlock them dramatically, if coincidentally. The individual forms were taken to symbolize war at sea (the water shard), war in the air (the vertical air shard), and war on the ground (the earth shard). The three shards offer a key to the product of war, and the resultant process of transformation for civilization. The Manchester skyline, itself severely blitzed in World War Two, is now punctured by the 55-metre-high vertical spire of the air shard. At the base of this is the entrance and from that point visitors can rise 29 metres to survey Manchester's surrounding land and water features, buffeted within the aluminium structure as if in a primitive biplane.

The main public galleries of the museum are housed on the first floor of the earth shard, a gently curving surface with one gallery for special, short-term exhibitions, and the other housing the permanent exhibition. The lower-slung water shard contains a restaurant and offices, in a prime position overlooking the canal and the quite different architecture of the Lowry Centre. Libeskind says that he builds in a world of order and disorder – he seeks here to explore the constant urban landscape of the 'in-between', given the spirit of

Above: Footprint of the museum on the site, with canal to the south

Below: Internal plan of museum

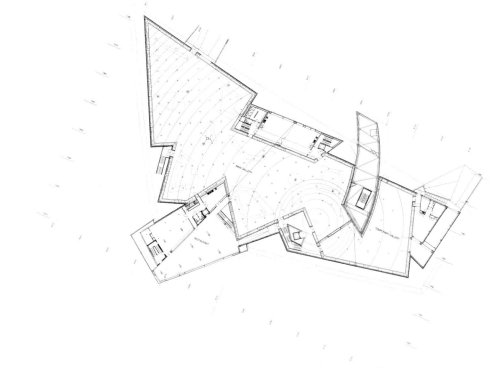

Above: The north canopy of the building, facing the ship canal

Above right: Main entrance on the south side. Paving is used directionally to articulate the entrances to the building

Opposite, above: The building seen across the neighbouring business parks

Opposite, below: Looking out across the Ship Canal

democratic openness, plurality and potential. A talented musician before he became an architect, he seeks references within the work of twentieth-century composers such as Schoenberg and John Cage, who themselves built on such values. The shards of the Museum now gleam in the northern light, glinting with the splendour of aluminium, a material developed for the contingencies of wartime. Magically, the building 'sings in the rain' as water flashes down its surfaces, glistening even under a dull sky. It is seen at its very best from the quayside entrance, especially if the visitor walks in across the new bridge from the Lowry Centre. A clever move has been to locate a small grey naval vessel next to the Museum. Like a seagoing vessel the Museum itself channels canal water through pipes beneath the curving first floor: sustainability applied to the cooling system, a typical Libeskind touch that converts raw technology into poetry.

This museum lies across the landscape memory of an older, nineteenth-century Manchester and so charts the tribulations of civilizations in conflict; yet this is done through readily accessible, authentic artefacts. These relics are the archaeology of war, significant in both personal and communal ways. The teamwork of architects and curators has enabled the central internal space to become something of a *mediathèque* by maximizing the projection potential of the walls and areas. The ancillary spaces are adorned with carefully selected hardware memorabilia, disposed

tentatively as in a time-capsule. Memory is plumbed more deeply by the 'push-button' accessible Time Stacks; here trays of selected objects appear in rotation vertically, behind glass in the traditional way. This material is thematically ordered.

Chronology is greatly clarified for visitors moving around the Museum in the conventional manner by a 'Time-Line' mural which creates a spinal pathway through the various fixed displays, treating distinct periods over the past century. Complementary to this are the silos which adorn the towering exhibition spaces. Such subjects as 'Experience of War', 'Science', 'Technology and War' or 'The Legacy of War' are well-crafted set-pieces in the great curatorial tradition, often seemingly archaeological in the presentation of the object, yet redolent of the great tide of war as it has swept across innumerable landscapes, scything through the history of different nations. This is tectonic building in essence, and yet its visual language seems closely affiliated to geology, time and permanent landscape values.

Igualada Cemetery
Catalonia, Spain, 1991
Enric Miralles & Carme Piños

For Enric Miralles, landscape and architecture were mutually generic, the product of the actual site concerned. It is arguable that at Igualada, Miralles succeeded in creating a total landscape which happens to contain some architectural elements. Various projects elsewhere have indicated the architect's tendency to assume a pre-existing landscape, and then embrace it. One example is Miralles' competition-winning scheme for the Parliament for Scotland in Edinburgh. This is currently under construction, despite the architect's death in 2000. The design is dominated by awareness of the volcanic landscape that long pre-existed the ancient urban community into which it has been fitted, albeit with some difficulty. Miralles' brilliant conceptual sketches bear this attitude out still further. The completion of the Scottish Parliament building will be a celebration of the climax of a brilliant career, suddenly cut short when the architect was in his prime.

Remotely located on the edge of Barcelona, Igualada Cemetery reveals Miralles' predilections. The work, largely completed in 1990, drew together many strands of original thought in a typology that has historically been dogged by religious convention, and even suspicion. There is a dramatic Modernist precedent, of course, in the work of Asplund and Lewerentz at the Woodland Cemetery.[1] Here, chapels and graves are beautifully positioned within a carefully nurtured Nordic landscape.

The key architectural elements deployed at Igualada by Miralles are the entrance, the chapel and the mortuary, accompanied by long rows, or walls, of burial niches set within a gradually descending, meandering way. On entry, the visitor is gently reminded of the fundamental essence of interment, within a clearly ascetic context. Whether one is in the realm of architecture or landscape seems irrelevant within such a focused generality. At the culmination of paths, the mausoleums stand firm, incorporated directly into the stone retaining walls.

Miralles was quite casual about the provenance of his inspiration. Later, curiosity might draw him to consider some reference to the relevant aspects of other modern masters. It is left for commentators, now deprived of any recourse to the architect, although his former partner Carme Piños is still practising, to explore whether in Le Corbusier, Wright, Kahn or Aalto there is something relevant. With Le Corbusier, it was the materiality of concrete that Miralles enjoyed. This enthusiasm may in part be attributed to the teaching of Moneo, Miralles' early professor. Le Corbusier's Venice Hospital has the semblance of a beautiful, water-lapped mortuary, but that is different, too. Alvar Aalto designed the Lyngby-Taarback Cemetery in Denmark with Jean Barouel in 1952. This is in some ways comparable to the Igualada Cemetery, but only to a limited degree. The ravine-incarcerated landscape which Aalto created for the dead did not deny the *Città dei Morti* idea (as Aalto referred to it) which traditionally enclosed all internalized accommodation within a dazzling white built-complex. Subtly and quite distinctly he established the burial ground proper outside this enclave, so as to embrace life freely. In the temperate Danish climate, Aalto's design fitted routes and paths within the opening of two equal, pre-existing ravines. The plan facilitated the tending of plants, almost on an allotment basis, while, as Göran Schildt comments, 'the purling, glittering presence of the "water of life" conveys an image of Elysium.'[2] Water was channelled along courses and conduits, supplementing the existing stream and natural drainage, slipping between the graves. Aalto replaced death with the cycle of life. That was a radical move in the lexicon of cemeteries.

Miralles, likewise, examines the cycle of time at Igualada. His cemetery is in essence one which also rejects the closing of the life cycle, the ultimate termination of the physical, so long expressed by cemeteries. Like Aalto, he disposes of the idea of the necropolis. For too long this city of the dead has been a metaphorical construct in the image of urbanity, miniaturized to reassure the bereaved over the centuries. Instead, going further than Aalto, Miralles pursued the time cycle of humanity back into prehistory, recessing the awareness of collective human existence to that time when only the primeval landscape of forest and cave could provide permanent sanctuary.

At Igualada, it is the idea of a sanctuary that seems most powerful. This does not mean that Miralles, by excavating this site, was denying the human need for identity of place. Traditionally, as Aalto also knew, the bleached-white wall surrounding the site fulfilled this purpose, conveying the same message as the sharp-profiled yews or cypresses, black in both sunlight and moonlight. Miralles uses the grouping and lining of strongly-growing tree species to the same end, to signify arrival, entry, and how to find a place. He allows these trees gradually to grow over the rockbound recesses, and he has nurtured within the hard landscaping a

Right: Site landscape plan of
Igualada Cemetery

Below: View down into the inner
recesses of the Cemetery

Above: Inner courtyard with tomb spaces. Note the patterned ground structure

Below: Conjunction of tombs and walls

Opposite: View down into the recessed tomb 'court'

softly pervasive ecology. In one sense, the site will never be complete, just as the cemetery itself must continue to provide new tombs within the structural frameworks provided. This carpeting of nature is achieved, unlike Aalto's model, without recourse to water features. It is a remarkable achievement.

In establishing topology structured by human paths, Miralles takes further a topological idea quite separately developed by Aalto. He designed the buildings pre-eminently around human movement in terms of crossings, clearings and connecting routes. This is a natural, instinctive and non-ritualistic progression. It establishes in the cemetery an idiom for freedom of movement, the freedom that seeks the beyond. So Igualada, too, draws the party of mourners, or the bereaved individual meandering down into a life-frame, past the simple opening with its vertical slanted crosses. The concrete curving roofs shelter the tombs from the sun, and the trees protect the mourners. Cemeteries are for centuries of use, and Igualada is no exception. But the

poetics are about life.

In any debate over the conjunction of architecture and landscape as one theoretical construct, the Igualada Cemetery could be seen as something of an archetype. Miralles has addressed fundamental considerations of form, typology, function and metaphor in a highly original manner. The mortuary roof, for example, represented a coalition of tree columns. It is as if a forest supported the roof itself. Elements will continue to appear 'unfinished', but since the whole dynamic of time is elided here, both built-form and land-form merge to predicate future form. The architect has gone, and Igualada now also stands as his perpetual epitaph.

1 Aalto in turn had been influenced by the work of the Swedish architect Gunnar Asplund (b.1885) and his colleague and collaborator Sigurd Lewerentz (b.1885) as exemplified in their competition-winning project for the Woodland Cemetery outside Stockholm. As Colin St John Wilson has said of Lewerentz's contribution there, 'here Lewerentz extended this experience of the confrontation with death to a much larger canvas, beyond the isolated 'chapel' building and out into the landscape at its most sublime.' Colin St John Wilson, *Architectural Reflections*, Oxford: Butterworth Heinemann, 1992, p.114
2 Göran Schildt, *Alvar Aalto – The Complete Catalogue of Architecture, Design and Art*, London: Academy Editions, 1994, p.62

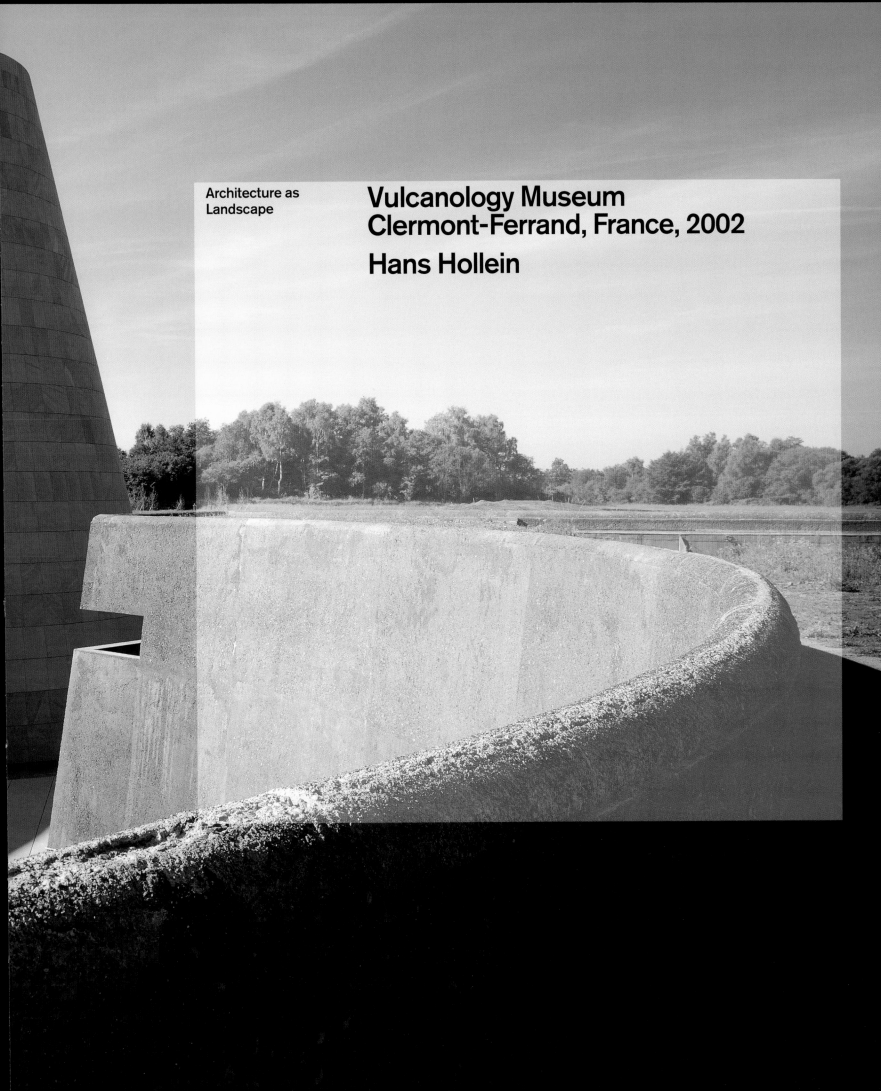

Vulcanology Museum
Clermont-Ferrand, France, 2002

Hans Hollein

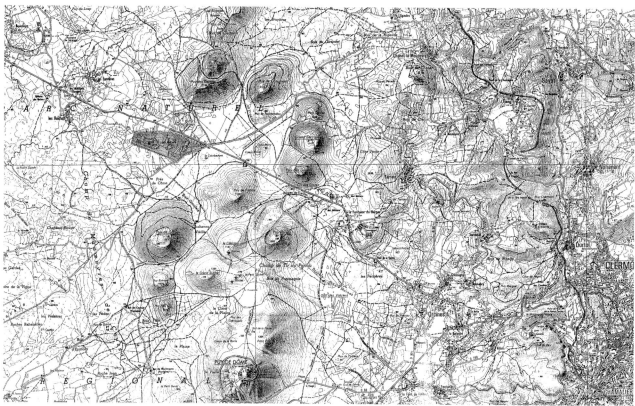

Right: Map of the St Ours les Roches area, showing the conical remains of volcanic hills

Opposite, above left: Sketch by Hans Hollein of the objectified place-form

Opposite, above right: The walkway at the top of the central courtyard

Opposite, below: The split cone above the entrance cone at the point of descent

In his Vulcanology Museum, Hans Hollein has established a dramatic discourse between the subterranean world and the merely terrestrial. The site is a famous volcanic landscape on the Laschamps plain in France. The original concept for the Museum was the inspiration of a former President of France, Valery Giscard d'Estaing, then President of the Conseil Regional d'Auvergne. His idea was to establish a new focus in the region of France with the greatest proliferation of extinct volcanoes. It was to be a combination of visitor centre and interpretation facility, a source of information about the volcano in a local and global context, a phenomenon that has both fascinated and awed humanity since prehistoric times.

As long ago as May 1994, Hollein learned that he had won the architectural competition mounted by the Conseil Regional d'Auvergne. Under the leadership of D'Estaing, this contest sought designs for an 'Espace Naturel des Volcanes' – literally a natural space for the existence and study of volcanoes. Some 86 architects had registered for the competition, including Norman Foster, Massimiliano Fuksas, Arata Isozaki, Richard Rogers, Ian Ritchie and Ricardo Bofill. Hollein was declared winner.

The buildings and projects that Hans Hollein has realized over the years fall into distinct groups. His other prestigious competition-winning design was for the proposed Guggenheim Museum of Art in Salzburg (1986). Although this was never realized, his plan to carve out architectural space from solid rock was a precursor of the Vulcanology Museum project. The plans show how Hollein's exploration of atectonic space evolved. Anxious to preserve the character of the historic skyline of Salzburg, he intended to build the

museum underground. At St Ours les Roches one can see this determined line of enquiry brought to fruition. The fundamental issue, as at Salzburg, was whether to subsume the entire scheme, sinking it in the landscape, or whether to recognize a need for some form of focus above ground.

The Vulcanology Museum project was contentious from the outset. The centre is located within a largely unspoilt, primitive landscape. A 'Save the Volcanoes' movement developed locally, with support from environmental groups. It was claimed that the project would become 'an ecological catastrophe which will lure fast-food outlets and cheap hotel chains to the foot of the existing volcanoes.' The new museum is prominently located below the most famous volcanic peak, Puy-de-Dome. A soaring, man-made cone opposite indicates the entrance to the underworld. From it a spiralling pathway leads downwards into the 'bowels of the Earth', through a 30,000-year-old crater with walls of volcanic lava. The space opens out underground to reveal various interactive exhibition areas. A Rumbling Gallery offers realistic simulations of volcanic eruption, and a car and buildings apparently engulfed by the magma flows. Then, by contrast, a humid volcanic garden appears, containing exotic plants such as giant ferns from New Zealand. This garden forms a kind of fulcrum. Leading off from it there are numerous video stalls. A Theatre of the Universe demonstrates how volcanoes were created.

The design brief had urged a clear 'separation between construction and landscape, not between underground and surface, and consequently neither between container and content.' The displays remind visitors of Jules Verne, of Dante's Purgatory, and of Plato's protective cave. Fire was to

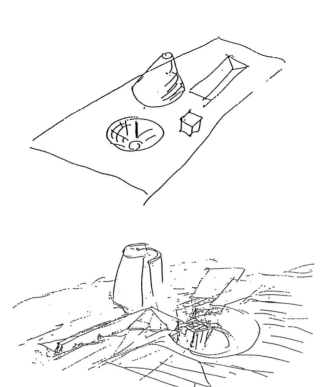

95

Above: The cone marking the museum, and the point of ritual descent into the Earth

Opposite, above left: Schematic drawing of the sunken volumes of the museum's main core

Opposite, above right: Spatial plan of the museum's main core

Opposite, centre left: The humid, 'volcanic' garden

Opposite, centre right: Local stone lines the approach way

Opposite, below left: Details of the entrance to the *cone doré*

Opposite, below right: Side view of the central courtyard

be present, the atmosphere was to be 'both sinister and threatening, but also exuberant'.

In all respects, Hollein's museum conforms to the tenets of Edmund Burke's definition of the sublime.[3] Burke himself quoted Milton's description of a place 'where all is dark and uncertain, confused, terrible and sublime to the last degree.' For the architect, this must have seemed almost unattainable in built form.

It is interesting to note that this museum is essentially a mechanism for descending into the landscape, so familiar and measurable above ground, so inconceivable below. Hollein designed the centre with the minimum of applied visual disruption (even in the actual context of volcanic schism, eruption and flow). His *cone doré* is an entrance marker, right down to its fire-ringed base. It also marks the location of the museum in a way that can be seen for miles around. In visual form, the cone is curiously eighteenth- or nineteenth-century, suggestive of an industrial tower. Without it, the centre would be virtually invisible to passing vehicles amid the ancient panorama of the mountains. To further enhance the sense of oneness and compatibility between the centre and the landscape, Hollein has deployed various types of local stone, combined with grass and water elements. Basalt, widely used in local vernacular building, is employed in several ways, both internally and externally. It appears either as a carved out surface, or as cladding in certain facades. Grass is also used as a roof-covering. The surface of the large viewing hall is composed of oxidized

copper, and that of the restaurant is of pre-polished lead, emphasizing the scheme's focus on materials.

Hans Hollein has recognized only the authentic realms of experience: no synthetic materials are allowed. He has emphasized the great difference between underground and surface textures, and for the visitor emerging into the bright sunlight there is the seemingly miraculous panorama of the immediate mountain ranges. Using all available information technology, Hollein has given greater meaning to the experience of man's natural habitat, 'the wild' in which this museum building is so carefully and intelligently sunk.

3 Edmund Burke, *Inquiry into the Origin of our Ideas of the Sublime and Beautiful*, 1756, ed. John Boulton, London: Routledge Kegan Paul, 1958, p.136

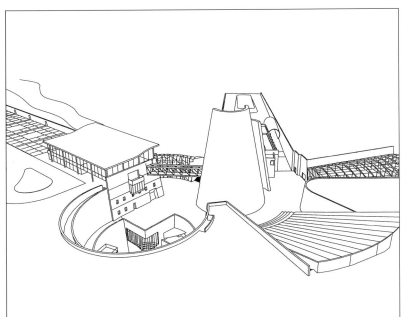

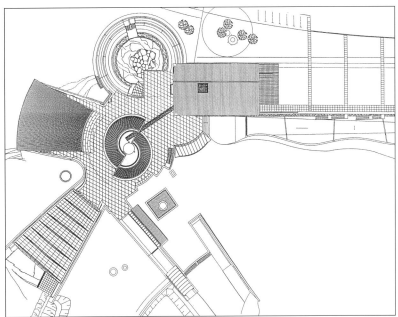

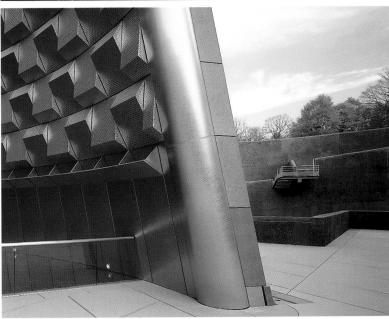

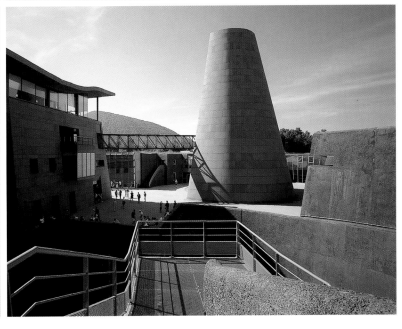

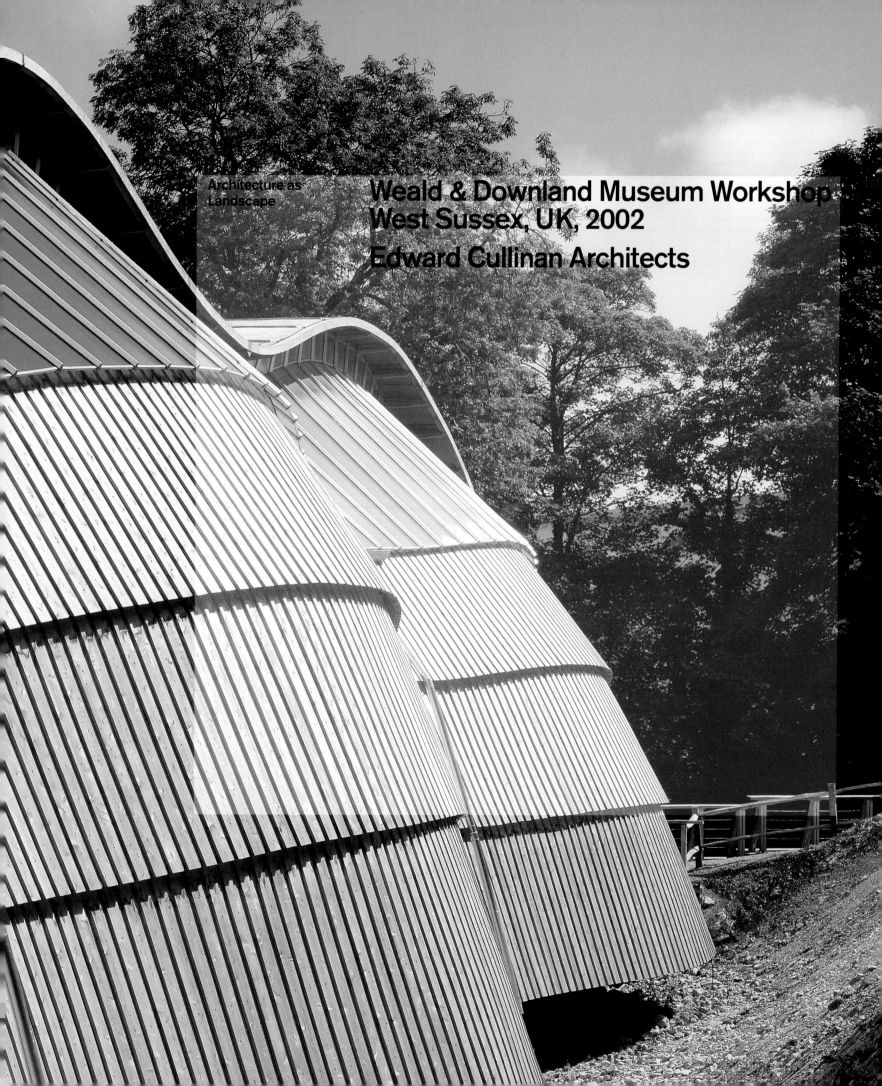

Weald & Downland Museum Workshop
West Sussex, UK, 2002

Edward Cullinan Architects

The undulating volume of the workshop gridshell fits readily into the landscape place-form

Set in a sensitive rural landscape, the Weald and Downland Museum Workshop is a dramatic solution to an architectural problem on a significant scale. The result was achieved by evolving a novel structural schema. Built using purely local materials and labour, it is the world's first permanent gridshell structure. A place-form has emerged that enables the host institution to express a dramatic new identity.

The 10-m (32-ft) high, 50 by 32-m (164 by 104 ft) workshop surmounts a 500 sq m (5,380 sq ft) masonry-built, earth-sheltered archive store, cut into the local chalk seambed. Cullinans worked with engineers Buro Happold to develop a gridshell as an appropriate basis, meeting all the contextual as well as functional requirements imposed by the brief. Cullinans themselves are established in the field of rural design: the Fountains Abbey Visitor Centre in Yorkshire is perhaps their most notable work.

The Weald and Downland project was for a new building, purpose-built to permit a full range of research, conservation and restoration to take place. The greenwood structure of the gridshell provides fully open access, and the place-form is entirely harmonious with the immediate museum complex of other buildings preserved for posterity. At the same time, the organic form literally 'rolls' along the site, reflecting, it seems, the undulating nature of the South Downs countryside.

The museum stands in a deeply historic landscape, well wooded since Saxon times. It is thought that the Romans failed to colonize this tract of southern England effectively, and its surface texture, land patterns and infrastructure still reflect the uneasy truce which prevailed. The prominence of the loosely-clad, clear-span workshop seems designed to reflect that ancient past. At the same time, the architectural solution is entirely contemporary; the structural format could not have been resolved without computerized design tools. As Cullinan says, 'it takes many years of high-tech building and computer modelling before we can go beyond it into the sustainable use of a minimum of materials from the forests around us.'[4]

The building, like its primitive predecessors, is identifiably tectonic, down to the earth-protected base for the sealed and sunken archives. The structure maintains the profile of a single-storey construct, although entirely two-storey in realization. Glue-laminated columns and a floor structure of laminated beams support a graded and sealed timber-plank deck. The building and site arrangements fully exploit the natural features there, such as earth mass through excavation, and natural flow rainwater collection. The gridshell itself is entirely timber-covered. Green oak lathes were obtained from England and Normandy. In design, the edges of the floor were naturally curved, allowing the lattice to form a characteristic three-humped gridshell, ensuring stability. Minimal supplies of energy are imported.

The architects, including Edward Cullinan, Steve Johnson, Robin Nicholson and John Romer, worked together with the Green Oak Carpentry Company, and with Michael Dickson, Richard Harris, James Rowe and Peter Moseley of Buro Happold. This close collaboration between architects, carpenters and engineers was central to the final character of the museum workshop. The collaboration brought a faint semblance of the medieval guild structure to the project, but the more modern benefits of high technology design tools were also available. Under a different set of circumstances, the architectural design process might seem to have been denied. However, the active involvement of the museum's directors ensured the realization of a place-form that was the expression of a harmonious, shared image.

It would be optimistic to say that the Weald and Downland Museum Workshop is the precursor of a new genre of sustainable buildings, that are at the same time contemporary and indigenous to their location. This is no metaphor for a local vernacular, offered *in absentia* to a remote community. Instead, it is a universally applicable philosophy realized in conformity with local needs, real rather than presumptive. The gridshell fits naturally within the landscape, rather than consciously dramatizing the place-form. Primarily, place-form here succeeds, where product-form will always fail.

4 Project description, Edward Cullinan, January 2002

Right: The two-storey structure is concealed by the lower level 'interrment in the soil'

Far right, above and below: The extent of the two-storey volume

Far right, centre: Section through gridshell over basement

Opposite: The internal workshop space, roofed by the gridshell structure

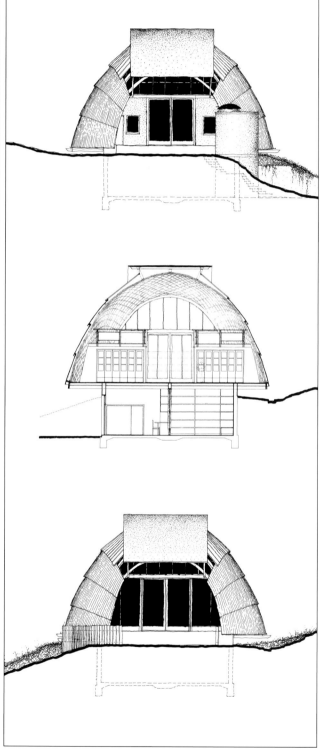

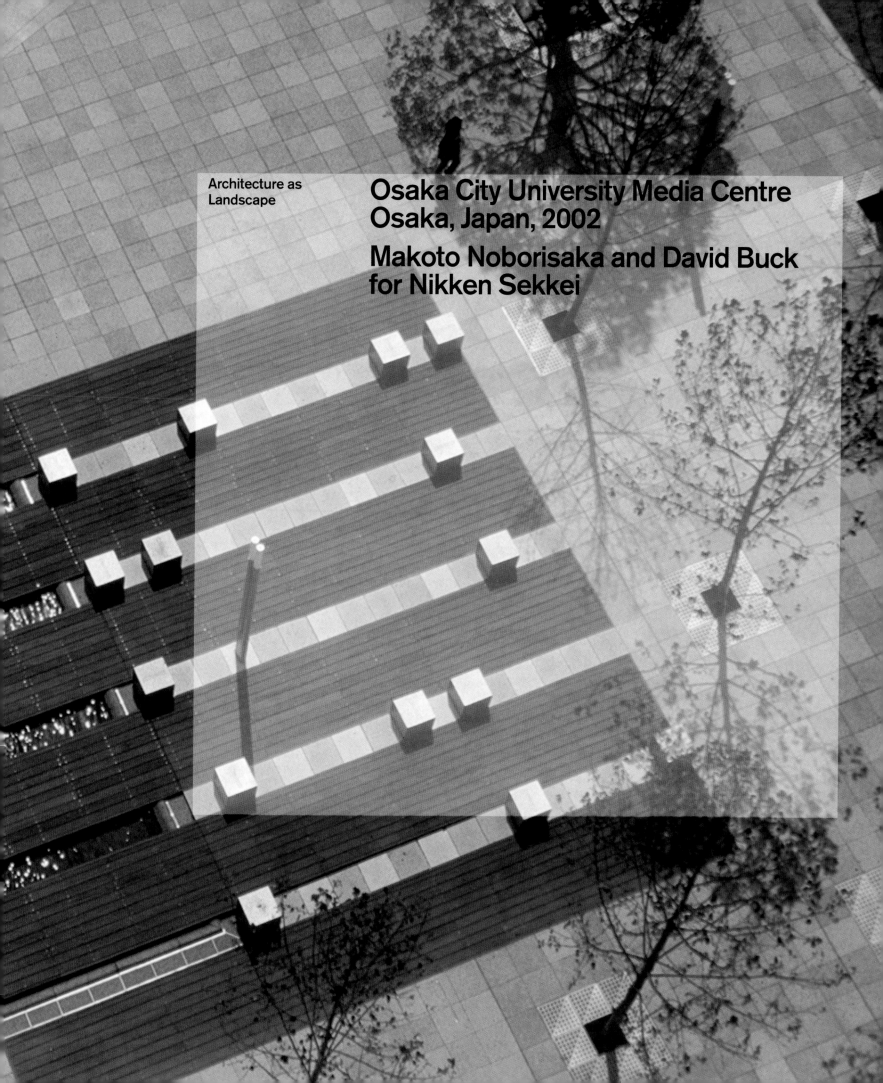

Architecture as
Landscape

Osaka City University Media Centre
Osaka, Japan, 2002

**Makoto Noborisaka and David Buck
for Nikken Sekkei**

Paved walkways emulate fractal landscape planar surfaces, and signify the disassociation from the architectural idiom as built

Noborisaka and Buck were initially somewhat challenged by the forbidding and rather uninspiring site. The architecture of the ten-storey, aluminium-clad building set on a neutral surrounding plaza was to represent the first phase of a master plan for regeneration. The arrangement presented to the landscape designers stood in marked contrast to the traditional pattern of universities in Japan, more usually revered as hallowed sites of learning. Noborisaka and Buck found themselves in a mediating role, standing between the local residents and the students who would be recipients of the intended benefits of such a plaza. The designers gave particular thought to the students, as distinct from the long-term residents, and sought to establish a liveable and comfortable relationship between both groups, given the formalized conjunction of library tower and surrounding landscape. In fact, it was the landscape design itself that would hold the key to achieving success or failure in an unrelievedly formal, hard-edged architectural context.

The landscape architects were given little scope for developing any kind of liberal planting plan, and yet a special sense of 'oasis' has been achieved. The aluminium canopy of the entrance to the tower was a bonus in this respect, mediating between tower and plaza in a way that was both elegant and dramatic. Yet it was the subtle deployment of water within the architecture of the plaza that really transformed the situation. What might initially have seemed to be some kind of ancillary addition to the vertical built form became the motive, poetic event. Since the architecture was generally less than significant, only well-disposed hard landscaping could create harmony between the space and the building.

Given the function of the library and media city itself – to transmit and access words – the landscape architects selected words from various library texts and dispersed them as concrete 'prose' around the plaza, scattered like *objets-trouvés*. Words, of course, convey images. Here the images sought by the designers were about landscapes of feeling, and landscape itself in the context of ecology. Aluminium name plates were cast, subtly and poetically infiltrating this apparently hostile terrain with the idea of nature. Arranged on a grid among the paving, grouped around benches or dotted around the pool amid the planting that did materialize, the name-plate words enable citizens and students to read together, thus acting as a kind of metaphorical link. The words also raise questions about the idea of nature, providing snapshots of man's knowledge and reconciling all this with the contemporary city.

The first group of words to be chosen was evocative of human interaction with the natural landscape. Drawing upon such reactions as awe, mystery, fear and illusion, these words sought to extract memories from earlier, more primitive times, of relationships with nature. The aim was also to elicit a direct emotional response.

The theme of words continued with a further 39 name plates that introduce the key concepts from landscape ecology, represented by mosaic sequence, species flow and the emphasis given to sound ecological values. Some plates were inscribed with the names of leading figures who have contributed to the study of ecology. Thoughtfully, blank plates were also included to accommodate their successors. For students, a tour of the name plates has become a kind of 'field trip'.

The library particularly requested a 'bookpost' that would permit students to drop in overdue books. The landscape architects continued to work within a metaphorical framework, coming up with the idea of an enlarged replica of Charles Darwin's famous *Origin of Species*, Darwin being the world's first ecologist. This aluminium compendium includes the complete contents, cover, title and even incorporates the paper texture of the original. Standing by the main entrance canopy, this work of 'concrete prose' clarifies the real function of the somewhat anonymous-looking building, and humorously highlights Darwin's historic contribution to ecology.

This remarkable example of ingenuity in landscape design arouses curious emotions. It is undoubtedly a garden where familiarity grows, breeding association and, in due course, a kind of personal attachment for those living and working nearby. As in all concrete poetry and prose, each individual forms in his or her mind a unique image derived from the names and words. This cannot be abrogated, but it is mediated by the rows of young flowering trees, by the fountains and the great pools. There is much to contemplate, not only at ground level, but also from the upper floors. The use of such an extended metaphor is not inherently Japanese, and yet it symbolizes the meaning of global culture, and hence the fragile global ecology to which the plaza is dedicated. There are few gardens, if any, furnished with words and names. For its originality as a solution to a problem, it is noteworthy, and as precedent it opens up further avenues of escape into the poetics of the garden.

Opposite, above: The massive block of the Media Centre and, to the right, the residential wings on the campus. Noborisaka and Buck created a landscaped distraction, using thematic applications of 'words' and water features

Opposite, below: Integration of waterscape with varied pavings enhances the over-view from the upper level of the surrounding high buildings

Above: Name plates set into concrete are dispersed around the plaza

Below: Detail of name plate and hard landscape surfaces

Architecture as Landscape

European Film College
Ebeltoft, Denmark, 1992

Heikkinen and Komonen Architects,
Landscape Specialist Jeppe Aagaard
Andersen

Plan and related
elevation/section conveying
relatively low density of site
occupancy. The plan also
reveals the compliance of the
various structures with the
geological 'flow' of the land
contours

If one is to describe architecture as idiomatic of the landscape, this is a very specific definition. Architecture can derive inspiration from the essential physiognomy suggested by the landscape of the site and its immediate surroundings. The buildings may become literally immersed in the landscape, or else display a plan and profile that integrates very closely with it. Alternatively, the architects may have acquired a survey of the land that records its salient characteristics, and may also seem to reflect the geological processes that shaped the form and structure of the underlying landscape.

The site near Ebeltoft is remarkably wild. It is almost a moorland, which must be unusual for a country as highly cultivated as Denmark. In some respects, the place has the characteristics of a grassed-over landfill site. In fact, the ground formations that have given the site its particular characteristics are the direct result of the Ice Age. The site contours actually convey the slow, monolithic dynamic of the glacial flow, and Heikkinen and Komonen have positioned the buildings to correspond to this dynamic. Glaciers tend to deposit very large rocks or blocks of stone, discarding them laterally as the flow edges forwards. Just as the shards and boulders of displaced granite are dramatically deposited in their native landscape of Finland, the building blocks here are laid down in riven deposits.

The site is wild, but it is also in the vicinity of the old town of Ebeltoft. This is an important contextual element. The deep valley on the site is left untouched. The largest block, wedged as an enfilade to the flow, is literally stuck there, penetrating the central ridge left by the ice. In an earlier version of this project, the accommodation buildings were grouped in a semicircle ranging up the contour. Subsequently this group was rotated in order to embrace the contour flow downwards. Metaphorically, one could see the 'flow' depositing this necklace of living accommodation either way around, to be discovered later like some archaeological find. The critical point is that the integrity of the valley has been identified and respected as a design protocol.

Such observations and descriptions can only really be tested and verified on site. This philosophy could easily be hijacked or abused by unscrupulous developers seeking to concentrate building volume, rather than follow a planning edict for dispersal.

At Ebeltoft, Heikkinen and Komonen have demonstrated the meticulous poetics of their practice. Over two decades, their work has displayed 'a poetic realism in the conception of architecture, one grounded in the knowledge of site, tectonics and light, but equally informed by experiences and sources beyond the defined formal discipline: the visual arts, cinema, astronomy, natural science.'[5]

Heikkinen and Komonen would claim to belong to the 'rational' Modernism that has long been recognized to represent a contrasting set of aesthetic and social attitudes of a professedly more Structuralist tendency in Finnish architecture, having diverged somewhat from the 'Humanist-rationalist' canon established by Alvar Aalto. Reliance on structural grids within the individual building envelopes has not, however, excluded a topological approach. It is simply that the essence of natural spaces in their minds is seen to obey a certain inherent structural dynamic, and so it is at Ebeltoft. This might be the antithesis of a romantic approach, but a reverence towards what is found is still common to both, and can be seen also to align with the painstaking observations of such artists as James Turrell, Hamish Fulton or Richard Long. Not for nothing have both partners visited Dolmen and Megalithic sites in Northern Europe, and studied the product of glacial flows or Native-American mounds.

A search for hidden geometries is predicated within the designers' own methodology. Stratum systems lying below contours might be one example, the product of longstanding planting systems or settlement patterns. Mikko Heikkinen says: 'Natural architectural spaces – man-made or nature-formed – often have the same effect. When you drive through the regularly planted lines of an olive grove you undergo an unbelievable kinetic experience. A ravine formed by nature itself, a stone cathedral, has a greater effect than most man-made monuments.'[6]

The European Film College harnesses such expediencies, and the structural format of the buildings themselves gives some evidence of a playing-down of the picturesque potential of concrete frames, which stand quietly adjacent to the supportive wall planes. The superstructure is used calmly rather than emblematically, to accommodate skylights and necessary external elements. It is as if the various buildings must simply convey their essential purpose; the various component blocks become embedded in a ridge, are scattered across a ravine, and preserve, where possible, the expanse of surface meadowland and rough, windblown grass and heath. In the middle distance lies the profile of the town of Ebeltoft and the edge of a wood. At the same time, every building's 'placement' is precisely calculated, both in relation to others, and also within the natural contouring of the glacial drift of the landscape.

The main block slices the site into two distinct parts, so the deep valley remains unbroken. An open terrace in line with the site contours faces back towards the student residences. Designed for recreation and relaxation, it is a kind of sheltered area in the fold of both the built structure and the unchanged site structure.

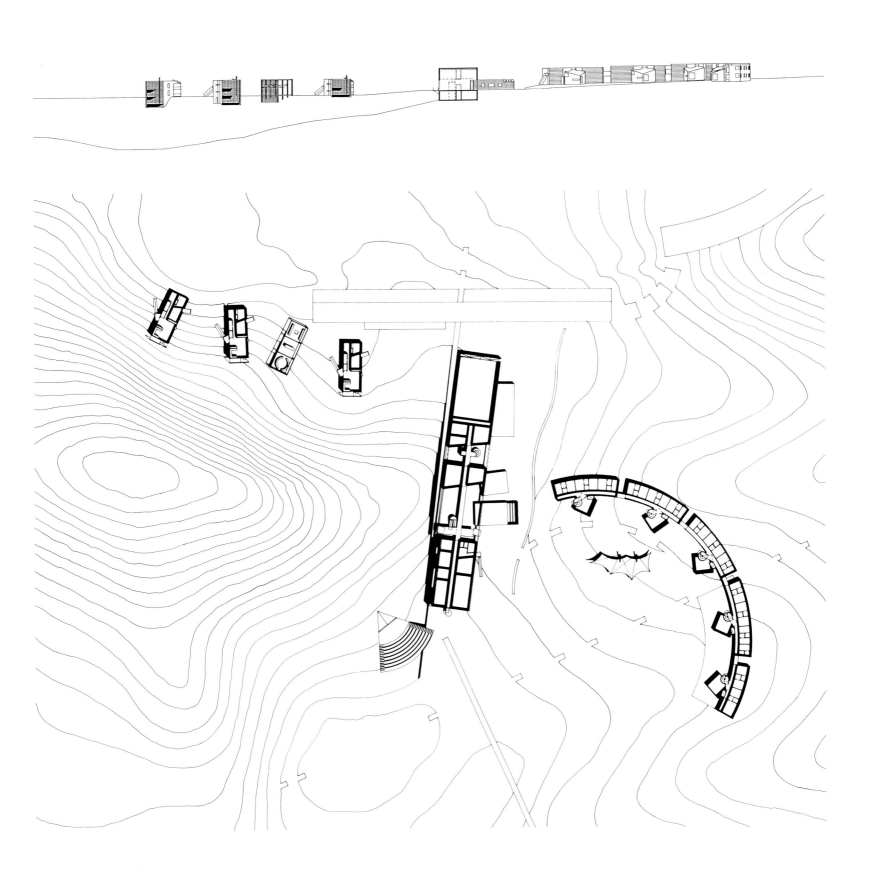

Above and right:
Accommodation buildings
maintain a low profile below the
skyline of the site

Opposite, above and below:
The skyline penetration of the
semi-circular block is carefully
contained, despite the
additional storey

The southern elevation of the building articulates small-scale necessities, built to the delicate scale of the town. Meanwhile the northern, 'cold' side has a stronger, more protective elevational treatment involving 3mm-thick zinc-coated steel plating. This is a fortifying armour (in an almost medieval sense) against the elements.

The car park area is set apart: an unbroken line that leads to the long entry bridge on the north elevation. This is cantilevered out over the natural valley, facing the distant skyline of town and bay.

The various buildings of the college have wide, glazed openings which allow the sense of landscape to penetrate through the building, leaving circulation spaces bathed in light. There is no artificial planting of trees or flower-beds; nothing disrupts the discreet collusion of buildings deposited here according to an agreed dynamic of a landscape essentially created some millennia ago. Appropriately, but perhaps surprisingly for a film college, there is no orchestrated architectural drama, but simply the *verité* of the landscape as found, with an adjustment of buildings as pure objects in space.

5 Project description, Heikkinen & Kommonen Architects, 1992
6 Peter MacKeith, article in *Korean Architects*, 130, June 1995, p.54

Architecture as
Landscape

Niigata Performing Arts Cultural Centre
Niigata, Japan, 1993–8

Itsuko Hasegawa

Overview of the centre, showing roof-level landscaping in green tracts co-ordinated with ground-level planting and the waterfront

Itsuko Hasegawa has succeeded in achieving the almost impossible. She has produced a design for Niigata that recognizes the substantial scale of the different components in this leisure-related building complex, and by enforcing a 'green' hegemony of natural landscape and planting, she has knitted the disparate architectural elements of the brief together as a single unified landscape. Given the pressures both upon and around the site, this is no mean achievement.

The architectural programme required a 2,000-seat concert hall with a separate 900-seat theatre, as well as a 300-seat traditional Noh stage. These key elements together comprised an 8-hectare site fronting on to the River Shinano. There were already some leisure activities existing on the same site, and the brief involved designing around these buildings. In fact, the project was somewhat compromised before Itusko Hasegawa even began to consider the possibilities for the new Cultural Centre buildings. There were also plans for a pumping facility to serve the area, as well as parking for 700 cars and the attendant roads. As the entire site occupied a reclaimed river bed, with a water table as little as a metre from the surface, all these facilities had to be located above ground.

The existing facilities were 'dotted' around the site with little apparent cohesion. However, Hasegawa recognized the way that older Japanese cities, such as Niigata itself, had developed naturally along such river-bed sites. The waterfront areas were not owned by anyone, and so tended to develop as anonymous spheres of public activity. Hasegawa recognized such random, multi-layered activity in her spatial concept for the site, referring to it as a 'positive fluctuation'. The design not only reflects the shifting winds and tides of the immediate locality, but also recognizes how such movement resonates with the musical rhythms of human life.

'Process city', as Hasegawa sees it, must also incorporate the collective memory. She seeks to impart a site ethos that is gently feminine, reaching for a softer, inherently positive and life-engendering philosophy. For example, it seemed as though parts of the existing landscape could be peeled off and floated over the infrastructure, ultimately ranged along the edge of the river itself. When Hasegawa discovered that Niigata had originally been an archipelago of floating islands, a fact concealed by urban expansion, she explored alternative ways to recover the inherent nature of the area.

Hasegawa conceived the new Cultural Centre as a series of floating islands. It was to be a retrieved topography, even though the three main halls had to be unified as one complex to economize on building costs. This concept has been carried through using a floating plate 6 metres above the ground. An atmosphere of lightness and transparency is created by an elliptical glass screen that 'wraps together' the

halls. Between these glass layers a retractable, perforated aluminium screen provides solar shading, necessary for an area frequented by the public. The sense of island 'topology' is enforced by establishing free circulation in a full circle around the core structures. An external network of bridges and gardens relates to the inside of the building, thus reinforcing the sense of a unified landscape that has been created through architecture. The whole site has become a performance space, with the bridges acting as part of the stages.

Hasegawa has always seen research into local history and conditions as a high priority. She says, 'land possesses certain dormant qualities in the same way that a human body retains memories of its origins somewhere within it.'[7] She has called this an architecture 'of second nature'.[8]

She believes that her designs come from 'a process of filtering the spirit of my own life in Tokyo'.[9] She would claim that the sensual traditions of Edo culture are still present in the physical and psychological spaces of her home city. She is quietly optimistic that the present, chaotic urban situation will be superceded by a 'new, higher dimensional space which will open up', rather than a catastrophe. Hasegawa believes that it may well be 'film directors or musicians or mathematicians or scientists' who can bring new order and freedom to Tokyo, rather than city planners.

Itsuko Hasegawa also likes to refer to molecular biology and the way it unifies all living things, including humanity. Yet she readily acknowledges that this suggests the abandonment of the idea of architecture as a product of reason. Nature includes total human life, 'accommodated as in a common ecology'. Such realizations became apparent with dramatic effect in Hasegawa's own work as early as 1990. Her scheme for the rejuvenation of Shonandai through the design for a cultural centre was a valuable precursor to the Niigata project. Hasegawa developed an all-inclusive flexible aesthetic, offering a multiplicity of solutions for a partially subterranean complex of auditoriums, gymnasiums, places for social interaction and a children's centre.

At Niigata, Itsuko Hasegawa's earlier research has stood her in good stead. She has remained undaunted by the apparently inhuman scale of development, and has brought to the project a fundamental spirituality about human culture and its related leisure activity, establishing a spirit of place in her new waterside landscape that continues quietly to resonate. Her work, as it has developed over four decades, is an exemplary precedent for female architects in urban design and landscape. Hasegawa brings a deepened sensitivity about place-making to the fore.

7 This and subsequent quotations taken from Itsuko Hasegawa, 'A Search for New Concepts', *Theory and Experimentation*, London: Academy Editions, 1993, pp.230–6
8 Hasegawa's text accompanying an exhibition of recent works, Aug 2000
9 Project description, Hasegawa office, 1998

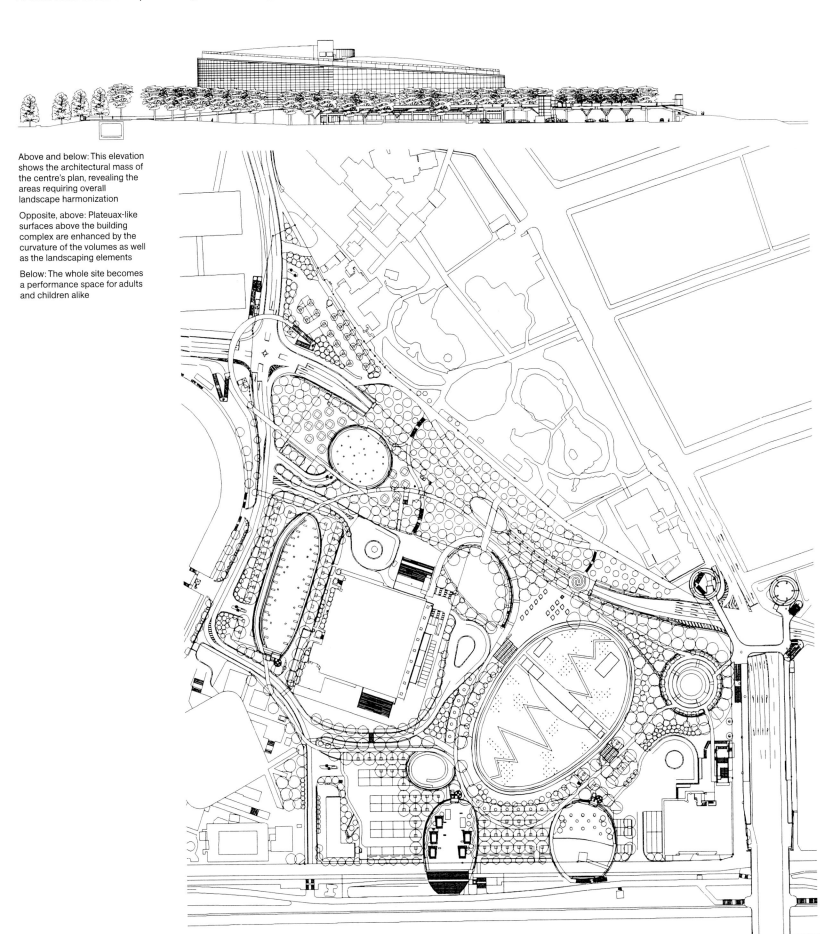

Above and below: This elevation shows the architectural mass of the centre's plan, revealing the areas requiring overall landscape harmonization

Opposite, above: Plateuax-like surfaces above the building complex are enhanced by the curvature of the volumes as well as the landscaping elements

Below: The whole site becomes a performance space for adults and children alike

Arthur and Yvonne Boyd Education
Centre, 'Riversdale' West Cambewarra,
NSW, Australia, 1999

Glenn Murcutt, Wendy Lewin and
Reg Lark for the Bundanon Trust

During the late twentieth century the architect Glenn Murcutt stood apart: he absorbed something of the Aboriginal sensibility and reverence for land and landscape and passed this on, through numerous house designs, to the broader Australian architectural community. His buildings sought not to root themselves in the Australian bush, but rather to 'touch the Earth lightly', in his own words.[8] Most of Murcutt's house projects have followed this basic idea.

The Arthur and Yvonne Boyd Education Centre at Riversdale, on the River Shoalhaven near Nowra, is built upon a happy coincidence. Arthur Boyd, perhaps Australia's leading painter (d.1999), gave the Australian people the site as well as the neighbouring property of Bundanon before his death. Boyd, who lived and worked here for more than two decades, displayed a profound reverence for the Shoalhaven river landscape where he developed his most dramatic paintings, chiefly focusing on sites damaged by mechanized leisure pursuits. There is here an element of Monet's Giverny, in France, a place famous for representing the preserved world of that painter. But Riversdale and Bundanon cover a much larger area of landscape, and include the various sites frequented by the painter.

This is a settled landscape, and yet the presence of the Aboriginal communities, with whom the land was originally associated, never seems far away on the ridged escarpments of rock and bush which overlook the settled ground and buildings. Overall, this is a site of exceptional topography.

Access by road is steep and somewhat forbidding. On arrival, one is presented with an almost Arcadian clearing. The old farm cottages where Boyd initially lived and worked once occupied this site. The ground then falls gently away to the river bank. Such was the scene first glimpsed by early settlers. Seasonal floods can transform the picture quite suddenly, an event often recorded by Boyd. River detritus, upswept trees and occasionally unlucky cattle float up-ended down the Shoalhaven reaches to the sea beyond Nowra. This was subject matter for Arthur Boyd.

Arthur and Yvonne Boyd's vision was to preserve for future generations of students and painters a world unchanged and undamaged by man. Murcutt and his team were given the task of designing a new building that would convey the essence of the place in all its moods.

The site was greatly admired by Murcutt and Lewin, who were joined by former student Reg Lark. They were dealing with a complex significantly larger than almost all Murcutt's earlier commissions. The centre was intended by the Bundanon Trust to provide teaching, drawing and painting on a communal basis, backed up by essential social facilities. There were to be up to 32 students at any one time. Murcutt developed a vernacular concept whereby the simple blocks of the traditional agrarian group of buildings, stockades and woolshed seemed important. The centre actually takes this

as its entry point on the north side. The new building nestles down, taking full practical advantage of the slope in order to incorporate two storeys at the point where the ground falls away more sharply to the river. The building topology as a whole is not immediately visible to visiting artists as they cross a wide, open terrace beyond the two traditional cottages that already stood on the site. Mushroom-coloured hard landscaping spreads at this point across a wide concrete plinth.

Murcutt recognized and took full advantage of the natural contouring of the immediate landscape. He also focused on penetrating ground surfaces with minimal impact: concrete foundations on piers reduce the cumulative effect of surface water flows. All waste water and sewage is carefully recycled and, as in numerous other Murcutt house schemes, rainwater is efficiently collected. Here it is transferred to underground cisterns for storage. The roof is corrugated in the normal way of Murcutt's rural buildings. It sits on a range of timber beams and is internally exposed. Simple doors, made for the most part of recycled timber, maintain this idiom. The terrace roof funnels the prevailing north-easterly breeezes into and along the corrugated roofscape.

Farm buildings here tend naturally to stand out from the surrounding bush and the centre is no exception. The building also expresses intellectual and artistic confraternity, with something of the spirit of the white stuccoed farmhouse that Boyd shared with a steady procession of fellow artists in Tuscany. Here at Riversdale the new buildings touch the site lightly, harmonizing a vernacular tradition with a widely varied site topography. In the opening expanse, a great canopy roof gives light protection of differing intensities throughout the daylight cycle, offering excellent conditions for painting. The window of each bedroom offers a framed and private view of the surroundings, near and far.

While this project underlines the reverence of one Australian master painter for his landscape, the place-form stands open to stimulate the creative urge of every visiting student and artist. This is literally a ballad of the locality, a visual rather than an oral tradition sustained. The centre sits tentatively facing the cultivated pastoral landscape of the later settlers, of meadow and river, so deceptively Arcadian, as they too found. At the same time, the ancient presence of the earliest Aboriginal hunter-gatherers is within throwing distance of the rear of the building, which lies partially embedded in the earth. This is a building for all seasons, architecture as homage, a landscaped place-form.

8 This phrase was used by Murcutt during discussions with the author in Sydney, July 1998. The idea is elaborated upon by Françoise Fromonot in *Glenn Murcutt: Works and Projects*, London: Thames & Hudson, 1999, pp.35–6. See also Vicky Richardson, *New Vernacular Architecture*, London: Laurence King, 2001

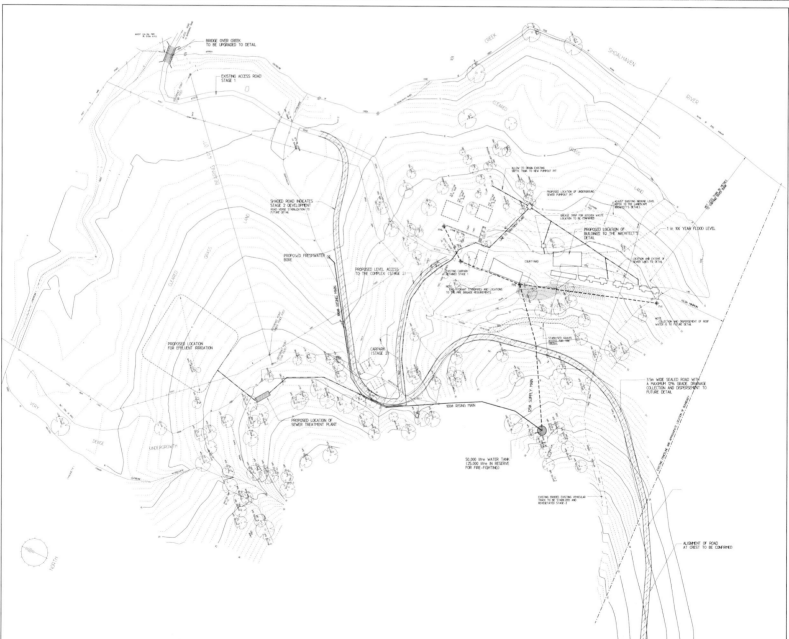

Opposite, above left: View from the edge of the bush landscape, showing the insertion of the westward elevation into open ground

Opposite, above right: Pre-existing vernacular buildings to the north of the new building

Opposite, below: Site plan with the new centre at middle right. The River Shoalhaven is at the top

Above and left: The centre's two-storey accommodation building, at the south of the scheme

Garden Landscapes

The most ancient Mughal paradise garden, the medieval pleasaunce and the great formal gardens of Chaumont, Chantilly, Villandry and Versailles all had one defining factor in common, that of separation from the wilder landscape beyond. By contrast, the English landscaped parks of Lancelot 'Capability' Brown frequently ran up to the walls of the houses they embellished, or were merely separated from them by a ha-ha, rendering the division imperceptible from the *piano nobile* of the mansion itself. The historical emergence of the villa gardens of the fifteenth-century Renaissance in Italy consolidated these differences.

Such Arcadian dreams were set apart and celebrated in ancient written and oral traditions. Ovid's *Metamorphoses*, the *Eclogues* of Virgil, and indeed the writings of Lucretius (*De Rerum Natura*) had been revived in the fifteenth century. In 1452, Leon Battista Alberti's *On Architecture* expressed an idea of beauty which 'arises … much more from nature, so that its true location is in the mind and in the reason'. His argument applied as much to garden design as to architecture *per se*, and remains largely valid today. Out of such an engagement of architecture with nature the Renaissance garden was born. Michelozzo Michelozzi's Villa Medici, Fiesole was a celebration of the dignity of learning and scholarship, enshrining Platonic values, restrained and harmonious in its combination of building and garden. Here, for the first time, Alberti's idea was realized in its purest form: a garden conceived in terms of its relationship with the surrounding landscape. The garden itself was a landscape of ideas. There followed the great French gardens which, in expressing power and status, far exceeded the immediate château surrounds in reaching axially for their distant landscape horizons.

A more interesting precedent for the modern landscape is possibly the Shinto or Buddhist garden. In research spanning forty years, the German architect Gunther Nitschke has contributed to the West's understanding of the unifying, rather than divisive, philosophy which has guided garden design in the Japanese landscape, bringing such precedent to bear upon contemporary design. Viewing Tadao Ando's Garden of Fine Art,[1] Nitschke reminds us surprisingly that 'it ultimately doesn't matter what art is exhibited here, European or Asian, sacred or profane; it clearly plays a secondary role to the art of space and place one is made to experience here over time.'[2] This example, a garden landscape constructed in a sunken void three storeys down in the ground, is a dramatic case of architecture in denial.

In the earlier twentieth century the garden landscape concept had become the *leitmotif* for Ebenezer Howard's emergent Garden City movement. Somehow it sanctified the idea of health in nature as a social antidote to the tubercular scares of the previous decades. For lower income groups in Europe, a solution was found: the individual family allotment of garden space, hemmed in by innumerable others on designated land. At Wedding in Berlin, Germany, the *Schrebergarten* is a series of allotments and habitable cabins.[3] The spaces are individualized, and yet essentially communal. The modern Jardins Familiales at Bron, Rhône, France are of a

The Jardin d'Ornement, or parterre garden at Villandry, Indre-et-Loire, France, created between 1906 and 1924 by Dr Joachim Carvallo

A *Kleingarten* at Wedding in Berlin (c.1930). A *Kleingarten* was a plot of land leased from the state and used by a familiy without a garden attached to their own home. A plot of this kind is often called a *Schrebergarten*, after Dr Daniel Shreber, who first spawned the idea

similar scale. On re-organizing the grounds to accommodate a housing estate, the authorities erroneously standardized the cabins, to the chagrin of the users, and the spirit of each individual plot was undermined. British variants usually maintained the right of the allotment holder to devise the 'shed', often from the flimsiest imported materials. In all cases, however, it was the combination of the individual urge to grow and recreate, with its organization on a mass scale, that led to success.

It is true that civic pride in the twenty-first century is very positively focused on provision for the pedestrian. Vergely, Mathieux and Berger's Promenade Plantée in central Paris has activated an obsolete railway route, turning it into a remarkable green filament which traverses the *arondissement*. Here, a continuous scenic panorama of the city offers diverse, impromptu visual experiences, not only of the grandeur and beauty of the wider skyline, but also of everyday life at a level above the street, so creating a series of episodic interludes.

Over the centuries, water has frequently played an important part in the garden landscape. From Mughal times onwards we find a continual reliance on water sources. In some two-thirds of the case studies in this book, it transpires that water features, natural or artificial, have been critical in the evolution of the final design. Among the Garden Landscapes defined in this section alone, three quarters incorporate water, either existing or introduced, as a defining element. Again, it is probably from Japan that the most profound recognition of the qualities of water has emerged over the centuries. Typically, the concept of 'hearing silence', as Nitschke claims, allows us to 'experience something of our own original nature, and beyond all form, and non-form'. Frank Lloyd Wright's Kaufmann House (1934–7), known as Fallingwater, certainly seems to invoke that Shinto experience; and even if his cascade dried up, the presence and remembered 'sound' would persist. Here was water's début as an integral part of modern architecture, rather than merely as an attached garden landscape feature.

Much later, at Hemel Hempstead New Town (1954), Geoffrey Jellicoe designed a landscape that incorporated a linear lake. Forty years later this garden feature was fought for strenuously by local users. Its removal from the landscape would have been an impoverishment of their lives.

Perhaps the fullest fruition of the urge to build with water has been West 8's ingenious creation (see p.170) on the two Amsterdam islands of Borneo and Sporenburg. Formerly container storage docklands, they have been transformed into a complete waterside habitat. Adriaan Geuze has here utilized the long bones of a harbour site to create a waterside garden of great individuality, at once historical and contemporary.

In Japan, at Kitagata, Martha Schwartz has established a unifying garden template within four separate housing blocks. Using water elements sparingly, she has established a recognizable harmony between buildings that are wholly divergent: landscape harmonizes all.

Both at the Jewish Museum, Berlin (Daniel Libeskind with Lützow 7) and in Toru Mitani's Novartis Pharma KK garden, garden landscaping is seen to fulfil its traditional role of enhancing the surrounding architectural scheme, mediating between building and surroundings. Kathryn Gustafson's beautifully orchestrated Esso Headquarters riverside garden utilizes water abundantly to provide a green sanctuary, anticipating too her competition-winning Princess Diana Memorial Fountain scheme designed for Hyde Park, London.

Bernard Lassus has created near Nîmes a Garden Landscape with a difference. Recognizing the needs of drivers and their passengers, he has provided both a series of separate, visual events and an oasis of peace where they can picnic. For landscape designers, the concept of the continuous garden landscape related to transportation infrastructure now offers a wholly new range of options, little exploited as yet.

The growth of the public's attachment to the qualities offered by design which adheres to historic precedent, while still operating within a chronological and global pattern of garden development, is invigorating. Where gardens such as Jellicoe's Kennedy Memorial at Runnymede traditionally incorporated mythology and illusion, such apparent fantasies as West 8's Swamp Garden at Charleston, South Carolina are seen to create a state of mind, in this case verging on the surreal, allowing the humidity, smell and natural textures of the location to create a total experience. Here no allusion is made, but reality is simply presented as the alligators float impassively by.

Historically, landscape architects have always been able to create both fantasy and allusion in presenting the garden landscape. The garden seems at first to locate naturally in Arcadia, but with this comes the demand for real sanctuary in the modern age, with security guards always near at hand. The original Garden of Eden provided Christendom with a compelling legacy. In biblical terms, the garden contained 'every tree that is pleasant to the sight and good for food'. In this respect the Islamic garden was wholly different, being contained within walls.

The modern antithesis of the Garden of Eden, with its multifold range of trees, is arguably the Parc de la Villette in Paris, designed by Bernard Tschumi (1986), in which Eden's trees are replaced by varied and stimulating metal structures. Tschumi fosters variety, pursuing the principle of 'heterogeneity', of multiple and disassociated, inherently confrontational elements all aimed at disrupting (perhaps legitimately) the 'smooth coherence and reassuring stability of composition'. Tschumi was to establish at Parc de la Villette a park that was anti-contextual and that challenged, many would say justifiably, the 'obsession of architecture with presence', the need to be meaningful or to signify. Tschumi would dismantle meaning as such, showing that it was never transparent, but socially produced. The humanist assumptions of style were suspect. Tschumi also questioned the term 'park' (synonymous here with Garden Landscape), asserting that it had 'lost its universal meaning, no longer referred to a fixed absolute, nor to an

Bernard Tschumi, Parc de la Villette, Paris, France (1986), not a *hortus conclusus*, and not a replica of nature

ideal. Not the *hortus conclusus* and not the Replica of Nature.'[4] Ironically, in seeking to remove such a proliferation of symbolism Tschumi might also be seen to refer us to the original ideal of untrammelled Eden, only subsequently enclosed with walls by medieval artists, no longer open to all species nor botanically correct.

Tim Smit's remarkable Eden Centre, designed by Nicholas Grimshaw & Partners, does much to provide botanical correctness, and despite the total enclosure of its world there is no aspiration to create Paradise as such, the centre being instead a dramatic invocation of the ecological and climatic basis of horticulture and arboriculture. In its offer of truth and clarity, it is in agreement with Tschumi's prescriptive demolition of allegory and symbol. Part of its success, despite its remote location, is that it quenches the thirst of urban minds for the reality and wonder of nature.

In the Parc de Conservation des Grandes Jardins in Quebec, the Canadian architect Pierre Thibault, apparently utilizing a point grid basis in much the same way that Tschumi did in Parc de la Villette, has produced an entirely different array of landscape installations. Primitivism is expressed, using a structure of disequilibrium. The so-called 'Winter Gardens' are intended to contribute to public awareness of seven mountain lakes. Thibault also seeks to amend our perception of landscape, with no alteration to the environment. There is no presumption to dislocate, as Tschumi found mandatory in the urban environment of Paris, but rather to engage the public mind. In both cases, however, a hitherto prescriptive attitude to the environment is replaced. Garden Landscapes fulfil a vital, multifarious and developing role again in the modern landscape, but only through such revisions can clarity and purpose be restored.

The Eden Centre, overview of biological site, temperate biome structures and walkways, St Austell, Cornwall, by Nicholas Grimshaw & Partners, 1998–2000

Pierre Thibault, Winter Gardens, Parc de Conservation des Grandes Jardins in Quebec (2002–3)

1 See Gunter Nitschke, *From Shinto to Ando*, London: Academy Editions, 1993, for a fuller discussion of this subject
2 See Gunter Nitschke, 'The Sound Silence of Water', in Michael Spens (ed.), *Landscape Transformed*, London, Academy Editions, 1995, p.20
3 'For a full discussion of this subject see Nicholas Bullock, 'Il Bertinese e la ricerca della natura' in J Rykwert (ed.), *Rassegna*, no.8, Milan, 1981, pp.39–48
4 Bernard Tschumi, *Cinegramme Folie, le Parc de la Villette*, Princeton, NJ: Princeton Architectural Press, 1987, pp.VI–VII

Garden Landscapes

Esso Headquarters
Reuil-Malmaison, France, 1992
Kathryn Gustafson

Opposite: The strong horizontal lines of the canals, inserted skilfully across the lawns, right, balance the mass of the headquarters building, left

Kathryn Gustafson has demonstrated an exceptionally prolific skill as a designer of gardens. In her own words, she 'works with the ground'. This approach is abundantly clear in her design for the Esso site, a purpose-built headquarters by architects Viguier and Jodry, where the gardens cover an area of some 1.3 hectares along the bank of the River Seine.

Kathryn Gustafson has divided the site with thin water courses or rivulets enhanced by willow trees and other naturally occuring species. She studied the orientation of the sun throughout the day, and then plotted the 'heavy' shadow cast by the building itself. Taking up the fixed points of both solstice and equinox, rather in the manner of Stone-Age builders, she was then able to plot the various orientations of the sun, and consequently the shade. This gave her the primary visual composition into which she introduced the parallel water courses, which are shallow canals. The waters run gently from an elongated upper pool with a simple paved terrace around its edge, bordered by steps. As a climax, a ramp leads down from the main entrance, connecting the offices with the River Seine and providing an area for walking and sitting.

Gustafson trained under Alexandre Chemetoff at the School of Landscape Design, Versailles which he founded in 1975. Chemetoff was the acknowledged leader of the movement of younger designers that emerged in the 1980s. He could also be described as 'the hero of the horizontal line in landscape space'. Gustafson is his worthy successor. She once worked in fashion design, and now she seems able to clad the landscape seamlessly, finding for each project a loose yet perfect fit. Her trademarks include the fall of light and shade across elegant contours, the poetic shading of green, and the precise control of water coursing which flows and eddies along the canals that she carefully designs.

In her design for the L'Oréal factory in Aulnay-la-Barbiere, France (1992), Gustafson wove together canal and shallow earth forms and folds, once again giving primacy to a single linear path with a footbridge. Her landscapes often work to redeem architecture of a less accomplished nature. Such gardens might be best defined as 'corporate greensward', all the more vital in such circumstances to redeem what stands as built.

It comes as no surprise that Gustafson came first in the competition for the Memorial Fountain to Princess Diana, on the Serpentine in London's Hyde Park (2002), as water is her supreme medium. This 'fountain' courses in a great, accessible oval, gently sloped to correspond with the natural fall of the site (see p.19). Since the Esso project, Gustafson has put in a full decade of practice as a designer, and it is significant that her work has remained immediately identifiable, formally consistent and wholly unique.

Above and below: Shallow gently moving pools and strongly geometric canals provide the dominant landscape elements on the site

Opposite: The powerful effect of the elongated upper pool, with its sloping ramp

Garden Landscapes

Garden of Fine Arts
Kyoto, Japan, 1994
Tadao Ando

Above: Ando's plan of the site

Below: Section reveals
concealed excavated levels
below ground datum

The Garden of Fine Arts was commissioned in 1991 by the Kyoto Prefectural Government. It was to be a unique celebration of the culture of fine arts within the broader context of Zen philosophy. It was also stipulated that the design should acknowledge the historical precedent established by Japanese architecture over many centuries. Given the passage of time, any culture less certain of its underlying criteria than Japan would have found these objectives virtually unattainable. Alternatively, the project might have descended, like so much contemporary Japanese and indeed Western culture, into kitsch, parody or make-believe.

The site of the Garden of Fine Arts adjoins that of a botanical garden, and functions literally as an outdoor museum for the contemplation of both Japanese and Western art. The reliance upon a kind of enhanced, visual simulacrum is an act of finely-tuned aesthetics that any European or American curator would find daunting. For example, a massive reproduction of Monet's *Waterlilies* forms the basis of a long, shallow pool. The images shimmer and glow in the refracted light of clear water, a vindication of all the artist ever intended. The meanings of such life-size reproductions as Leonardo da Vinci's famous *Last Supper* also seem enhanced by access through such a tranquil garden environment.

The Garden of Fine Arts displays an awesome perfectionism that inspires visitors, for nothing is lost through the fusing of garden landscape and work of art. For Ando, with his complete absorption in issues of landscape and the materiality of the elements, this garden represents the consummation of many long-held ideals.

Entering the garden from the Kitayama Road, the visitor immediately reaches the conclusion that this is neither building, as conventionally realized, nor garden *per se*, but some magical fusion of both. The excavation of the site to a depth of three storeys creates an impressive geological and topological feature, which makes its own, independent impact. In Ando's own words, 'an enclosed area is prepared below ground level within which three walls and circulation consisting of bridges and ramps creates a rich variety of spaces on three levels. Water is introduced into the experience through three waterfalls and pools at each level.'[1] Ando adds that he seeks to create the experience of 'a contemporary volumetric version of a stroll garden'.

Ando's acute sensitivity to man-made materials is well known, and one might have expected him to return to the luminous effect of the timber-built Buddhist temple that he designed for Komyo-ji, the Pure Land sect of the religion. But this presumption underestimates Ando's attachment to concrete as a building material.

Upon entering the Garden of Fine Arts, visitors encounter pools on both sides of the route. On moving forward, the path runs along a very thin concrete walkway. The visitors' perception is then altered by Ando's use of Monet's painted flowers underwater. They begin to see as children do, abandoning the cherished conventions of fine art.

By using ceramic reproductions, Ando has removed the constraints of weather and climate, creating a collusion between indoor and outdoor space. Historical and more modern images are re-created by impeccable photography, then transposed to ceramic panels and finally subjected to industrial firing. These colours will never fade or lose tonal impact. The process of transcribing the 'positive' of the painted image plate directly on to a ceramic board (itself subjected to the chemical process of calcination) results in total accuracy. Numerous plates are joined together to form the full representation of the painting. Leonardo's *Last Supper*, for example, is made up of 110 plates, each measuring 60 cm by 3 m. To view this, one must stand almost ritualistically on a sharp promontory overlooking a landscape of waterfalls. It is important to understand the importance that Ando attributes to the positioning of works of art within a given spatial continuum, whether religious or secular. This is characteristic of a wide range of Ando's work, where interior and exterior environments appear seamless. He takes the element of water, for example, and allows it to define its own space.

Ando is careful not to disorientate the visitor, although he always retains the vital quality of surprise in the landscaped sequence. Accordingly, raw concrete is always used for the walls that run parallel to the visitor's movement. The orthogonal is always denoted by the device of a waterfall. The water cascade, however, is deployed differently; head-on, full frontal, it is as if one goes under the platforms of cascading water, moving now up, now down in harmony with the spatial concept. All one's physical senses become involved – sight, hearing, smell and touch – in another world from the everyday. Ando establishes the permanent presence of the garden landscape, mindful of its history as a genre, but in an entirely new mode.

1 Project description, Tadao Ando, 1994

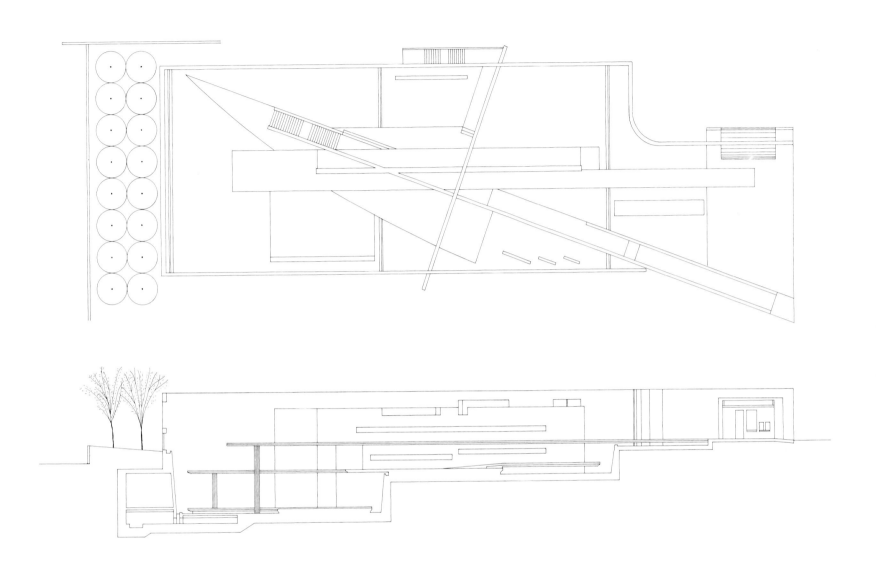

Opposite, above: The primary axial walkway leading from the Kitayama Road

Opposite, below: Relationship with a re-created masterpiece: generous gallery space for viewing the entire work is provided

Left: The return route between the works

Garden Landscapes

Jewish Museum
Berlin, Germany, 1997–2001
Studio Libeskind with Lützow 7

An enclave for play in the garden re-entrant of the Museum. Note the treatment of the hard-landscape paving

Cornelia Müller and Jan Wehrberg were instrumental in designing the environment around the Jewish Museum, Berlin, which was conceived by Daniel Libeskind. Their design philosophy focuses on the discovery of specific characteristics relating to a particular architectural scheme. Denying self-reference in their work, they avoid their own design stereotypes. This self-effacing method made them particularly suited to collaborating with Daniel Libeskind, whose design idiom is immediately identifiable.

Before working with Libeskind, they had already revealed both participatory and ecological leanings in their work. Chasing a new identity, they called themselves Lützow 7, and developed the idea of a narrative format, the equivalent of the 'storyboard' in film. They had already worked with Libeskind on the Felix Nussbaum Museum in Osnabruck, and a *modus operandi* had developed. This prior collaboration stood them in good stead for the more complex Berlin project.

Based in Berlin, the designers knew the city's culture, and its obsessions. This assisted in the formulation of a new narrative, working deep within the 'grain' of the city. In a previous project in Berlin, commissioned by Axel Schultes at the Federal Chancery, a more conventional and institutional formalism had been required. Projects for the Federal Ministry of Labour and Social Affairs, and for the Ministry of Economics and Technology, also in Berlin, followed similar edicts. At Osnabruck, the Libeskind designs had demanded a landscape that would reconcile an existing villa with the triangular disposition of space in the new building. This also involved the sculptural integration of an ancient bridge found on site. Although simpler in form, this project could be said to anticipate the greater complexity of the Jewish Museum.

At the Jewish Museum there was an existing Baroque palace to connect with, as well as a modern garden behind the building. The designs for the external environment by Müller and Wehrberg embrace and wholly reflect the idiom of the Jewish Museum as established by Libeskind. The landscape designers have ensured that no visual or perceptual break occurs between inside and outside. The Museum itself seems borne out of historical genesis by conflict. Seen from the tall apartment blocks nearby, it is like a meteorite, impacted dramatically upon the open site. Ignorant of the streetline, by conventional town-planning rules it would appear to have nearly missed the building line, projecting across into the road. This is all intentional, as is the contrived slant which the E T A Hoffmann garden reveals as it tilts towards the Museum.

In the Jewish concept of making places, 'the Deed, the Word and the Thing' are explicit and irrevocable. The slanting, formalized concrete columns of the Hoffmann garden mediate behind the entrance, extending the symbolism with which the Museum is enriched. Each of the 49 columns is surmounted by an oleander plant, all of them now growing well and firmly established. The block of seven by seven columns is dramatically displaced from the Museum itself, as if they were somehow detatched on its impact with the earth.

Libeskind's philosophy provides a narrative across the site that is then interpreted by Lützow 7. It is summed up in the verbal notation that he concocted to describe it: 'Between the Lines' is essentially the *leitmotif* here, handed to the landscape designers.[2] The linear representations of this idea in both hard and soft landscaping are skilfully established by Müller and Wehrberg. Since Libeskind's building 'footprint' conclusively avoids the orthogonal, even the rectangle as such (in the same way that it rejects any concept of 'facade'), a number of acute-angled, re-entrant spaces occur. These are detailed to concur with the underlying narrative. Directional guidelines run across the surface of the landscape plan, along which future activities might occur. Further away from the building, a small group of false acacias with dark trunks has been inserted. This group seems to represent a reversible notion of 'paradise', becoming an idealized 'wilderness' abounding in the garden of presumed civilization. Through the trees snakes a rill, a kind of serpent of mythological significance.

The Paul Celan courtyard is another area of special and significant focus which fits into the second re-entrant space formed by the building. A drawing taken from a work by Gisele Lestrange Celann is replicated in the patterned pavement of the courtyard, where fragmented linear forms are fully incorporated on the ground.

Lützow 7 undertook a major responsibility when they began to interpret the architectural brief as landscape. Their role here was essentially one of inventive reconciliation. The building itself made a dramatic impact on a site that had been derelict since it was bombed during the Second World War. What natural, ecological growth had been achieved from the ruins of the past was sustained in practical terms. The two key garden insertions, described above, were linked by the 'fault lines' of the paving system. Elsewhere, too, a Jerusalem rose blooms, for the future as much as for the past.

The landscape project for the Jewish Museum demonstrates unequivocally the successful fusion of architecture and landscape design, achieving the full reconciliation of architecture and site surroundings within a wholly urban context.

2 Donald L Bates, 'A conversation between the lines with Daniel Libeskind', *El Croquis*, 80, Barcelona, 1996, p.6

Right: The design correlation of building, tree and lawn layouts

Below right: The street view of the well-planted tree garden

Opposite, above: The E T A Hoffmann garden, with the oleanders already well established on the summit of each column

Opposite, below left: The cohesion of zinc cladding and natural, deciduous trees

Opposite, below right: The landscape harmonization of the E T A Hoffmann garden, other planted areas and the Museum elevation

Garden for Novartis Pharma KK
Ibaraki, Japan, 1993
Toru Mitani

In this substantial garden designed for the Novartis chemical complex, Toru Mitani has established parity between buildings and landscape. Few other landscape architects would have been able to balance the demands of such a massive building. Mitani, however, was quick to resolve the apparent dominance of the complex by establishing quite categorically an 'inside' space and an 'outside' space, an inner courtyard and also a formalized exterior domain. This exterior relies upon a combination of formal planted avenues with corresponding linear water features which combine to exclude invasive car parking. From inside the courtyard a diagonal is thrown across the space, and this geometry is parried externally by a circular area of 'two-tone' planted ground cover.

Mitani is arguably the leader of a new generation of Japanese landscape designers. Born in 1960, he first trained at Tokyo University as an architect, also completing a PhD. there. He turned to landscape as a reaction to the seemingly endless stylization of Postmodern architecture, moving to Harvard University in 1987 and following up with a stint in the office of Peter Walker and Martha Schwartz.

On his return to Japan, Mitani found himself increasingly concerned by the extent to which civil engineering projects had been slicing through the delicate fabric of the Japanese countryside. 'Earthworks are not simply a matter of regulating space by the shapes which are apparent on the surface of the land,' he said, '…it's the invisible things such as methods of drainage, the composition of the soil and the structure of the land below the surface that in reality decide the quality of the spaces on the face of the site.'[3]

The design for Novartis Pharma in 1993 was Mitani's first large scheme, laying down a pattern for his future work. It was followed by a series of projects, including the much-praised Kaze-no-Oka Crematorium Park in 1997. This design relied on simple, formal layouts seeking to recover, as Mitani says, that intimate contact with the Earth itself.

Mitani developed a technologically-based landscape modernity as an antidote to all-pervasive Postmodernism. In his own words, 'I couldn't see any hope in such a design attitude, so I decided to escape from Tokyo to the United States, escaping the endless quotation, endless manufacturing of vocabulary, form and sign.'[4] While in the United States, Mitani was profoundly impressed by visiting Michael Heizer's *Double Negative* (1970) in Nevada. He was struck both by Heizer's own manipulation of technology and by the scheme's generation of a sense of place.

Generally, Mitani expresses a bias towards a truly 'functional' landscape architecture, accepting the increased scale of operations that technology facilitates. One of his trademarks has been the use of pure white elements to emphasize formal definition, enabling meaning to be clearly read. There is, of course, some affinity between Toru Mitani's work and that of his mentor, Peter Walker.

Wherever feasible, Mitani employs technology to access the ancient traditions within the history of landscape and gardens, which are a source of inspiration and spiritual meaning to him. He also seeks to mitigate the rules of chaos, and to utilize the Modernist spatial precedent as a kind of compositional tool, in order to foster the sort of landscape that is facilitated rather than inhibited by technological progress. Mitani's work shows a particular sensitivity to spatial corollary, to systems of counterpoint, and their potential to mediate the overwhelming presence of large contemporary buildings. He believes that landscape's role is also assisted by 'quietness and simplicity', and that the concept for any scheme can be simultaneously silent and clear.

Back in 1993, Mitani worked with Studio on Site, and demonstrated consummate skill in establishing for YKKR+D a major roof garden, in Tokyo, where the bounds of landscape design and installation art seemed to coalesce. The client had asked for a sculpture in steel to be placed outside the presidential offices. Mitani very subtly avoided inserting a single object work, which would have created a single focus. Instead, he concocted a remarkable matrix of 44 'wind fish', a multipartite, dynamic weather vane. The shoal of fish swims in whatever wind currents pass the site, bringing natural motion to the office outlook. This scheme is an outstanding demonstration of the ability of landscape architects to enter the realm of installation art, although few of them manage it. Mitani brings new dimensions to landscape architecture, and revalidates the traditional role of the garden designer.

3 Quoted in David N Buck, *Responding to Chaos: Tradition, Technology, Society and Order in Japanese Design*, London: Spon Press, 2000, p.57
4 Ibid., p.56

Above and below: Tree planting is both 'natural' as in this bosquet, above, or follows a strict geometry, below, in avenues on the longitudinal axis to the site

Above: An overview of the
Novartis Pharma complex,
showing the inner courtyard and
the exterior landscape scheme

Below and opposite: Details of
the planting in the formalized
external and internal garden
areas: tree planting, the circular,
external grass lawn, the long,
axial canal and formal internal
lawn

Garden Landscapes

Kitagata Garden City
Gifu, Japan, 2000

Martha Schwartz

Above: Inside one of the boxes that make up the Four Seasons Garden at the eastern end of the site, children make use of the enclosed but open-roofed space to play

Below: With Diller + Scofidio's building forming a wall to the northern boundary of the central spine, the Stone Garden (left) and the Four Seasons Garden (right) form just two of more than a dozen discrete landscape areas

The Garden City became established in Europe during the twentieth century, following the pioneering experiments of Ebenezer Howard in Britain. It has no such precedent in Japan. This is in part due to the fact that social housing in Japan is not the recognizable entity that it is in Europe. Although the rows of medium-rise, high-density living accommodation owe a token debt to established European criteria, such as daylight factors, the resemblance is otherwise very limited. At Kitagata, in Gifu Prefecture near Nagoya, steps have recently been taken to remedy this deficit by establishing a model for the future. The innovations could serve as an example to European local authorities and private developers alike. The architect Arata Isozaki has initiated the concept prototype, which was strongly promoted by the Governor of the Prefecture, Taju Kajiwara. It is perhaps because Kajiwara is a trained engineer, with a special interest in the social aspects of architecture, that it has been conceived in such an original way. Firstly, four architects were invited to draw up designs, each for a separate apartment block. All of them were women: Elizabeth Diller from the United States, Christine Hawley from Britain, Akiko Takahashi and Kazuyo Sejima from Japan. The landscape architect Martha Schwartz was invited to take design responsibility for the entire exterior surroundings of all four areas. In other words, it was the garden landscape design that would unify the entire scheme.

There was yet another unusual but ingenious condition: none of the four architects was allocated a site. Each was to prepare a highly detailed scheme without direct reference to a specific plot in the designated site. These conditions might have produced a fragmented outcome, but that would be to reckon without the unifying role of the landscape architect. The designs could be expected to be compatible, because they would all meet the high standard to be expected from such architects. The idea was to generate a range of alternative solutions and a discrete cultural mix, a condition which Ebenezer Howard's pioneering British schemes failed to supply, and which, in the 1960s, Jane Jacobs came to

recognize as vital to city living.[7]

Martha Schwartz's role was to form a creative symbiosis by means of landscaping the entire external area. Unusually, therefore, a decisive design responsibility was being placed upon the landscape architect.

Martha Schwartz's landscape had to be based on the apartment block designs submitted by the four architects. Elizabeth Diller, for example, devised a flexible internal plan based partly on the well-proven precedent of the New York City loft. Covering the northeast section of the site, Diller's plan now angles southwards in a very gentle curve, in contrast to Takahashi's block which runs westwards on the east–west axis. South of this, Christine Hawley manages to break with the orthogonal axis, allowing her duplex units to face southeast or southwest. Kazuyo Sejima fills the southwestern section of the site, creating a long corridor in the manner of the Japanese iniwa (garden passage). The passage serves a series of linearly-disposed rooms. By establishing an 'elbow' she achieves a sense of enclosure, forming an 'inside' and an 'outside' to the block.

The manoeuvres of both Hawley and Sejima, following the final site allocation, allowed Martha Schwartz herself considerable latitude in formulating a diversity of landscaped areas. The exterior boundary of the site is generously planted with trees in rows of varying depth.

Schwartz established a strong central spine on the east–west axis, where the dispositions of the four architects had created an indeterminate, fairly wide but somewhat vacant wedge of intermediate space. Essentially, Schwartz converted this space into a suite of interconnected garden rooms. She created a wide variety of small, human spaces, almost like beads on a string. There is, for example, a long pond dubbed the Iris Canal close to Takahashi's linear block. There is also a Stone Garden, where rocks and fountains define a playpool. At the eastern edge of the layout there is the Bamboo Garden, and four specific enclosures known as the Four Seasons Garden. These are animated by a rill of water and planted with trees that mark the changing seasons.

There is a dance floor, orientated west to catch the evening sun, and a sports court, close to the rill. These features combine to enliven the central axis.

Given the format of covered car parking arrangements below ground level, Schwartz was able to raise the level of the long central spine to create a kind of 'dais'. The apartment blocks are occupied by a wide range of demographic groups, and as a result the central dais is used for a variety of activities by individuals and groups. It is 2.5 metres (7.5 feet) above actual site datum level, which makes sense on a site without any ground-level living accommodation.

The twelve different garden rooms provide a unique range of flexible spaces. They are used variously as enclaves, openings, walkways or places in which to simply stand, sit, watch or contemplate. There is no precedent for the design in Japan, Britain or the United States, the home countries of the four architects.

Kitagata Garden City is a remarkable scheme. It demonstrates the special unifying force of landscape design. Schwartz has shown how both hard and soft landscape elements can be combined with water features to bring unity to an entirely new community.

5 Jane Jacobs, *The Death and Life of Great American Cities*, New York: Random House, 1961. This seminal work alerted planners and architects to the fundamental concerns of city growth

Far left: The Iris Canal

Left: The Willow Court and the Iris Canal

Below: Plan of western end of the landscaped spine

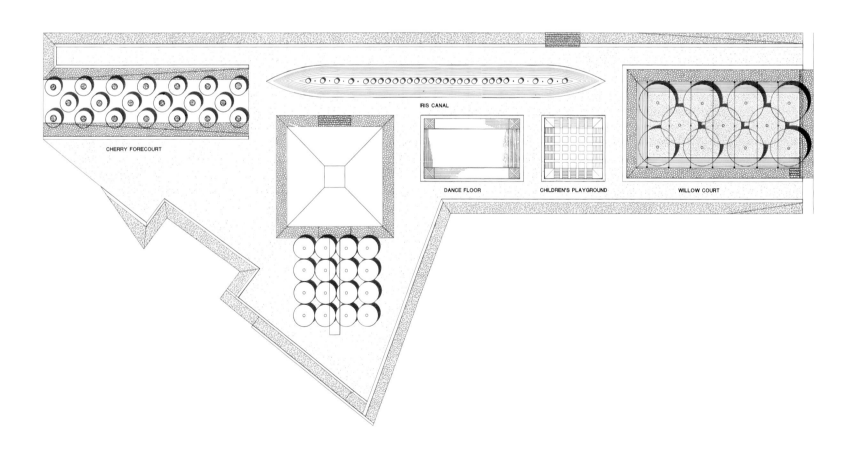

CHERRY FORECOURT

IRIS CANAL

DANCE FLOOR

CHILDREN'S PLAYGROUND

WILLOW COURT

Far left: The Stone Garden

Left: The Four Seasons Garden

Below: Plan of eastern end of the landscaped spine

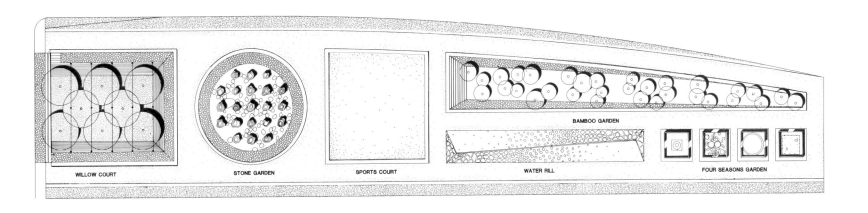

WILLOW COURT   STONE GARDEN   SPORTS COURT   WATER RILL   BAMBOO GARDEN   FOUR SEASONS GARDEN

Garden Landscapes

Borneo Sporenburg
Amsterdam, Netherlands, 1998–2001

West 8

Above: The container port
before redevelopment

Below: The port following
redevelopment for housing.
Note the new pedestrian bridge
to the right of centre

One of the most unusual aspects of this project was not generated by West 8, the landscape architects of the masterplan, but by the City Council of Amsterdam. Perhaps for the first time ever, a firm of landscape architects were winners in an urban design competition. They were rewarded with both the project brief and the absolute confidence of the local authority.

The competition covered the Borneo and Sporenburg peninsulas in the eastern sector of Amsterdam's commercial docklands. The area had already been the subject of a demanding housing brief requiring some 2,500 housing units to be built on a low-rise basis, with a density of 100 units per hectare. Over 100 architects actually contributed to the planning parameters, each creating a prototype dwelling. Ideas were shared in multi-disciplinary workshops held during the final planning stage, and with the involvement of the public. Five main, yet differing, typologies were devised for the housing.

Architects such as OMA and Claus en Kaan were each invited to contribute a dramatic 'sculptural' block as a visual event, and De Architekten Cie-Frits can Dongen also contributed a dramatic 'whale' apartment block. The real poetry and cohesion of the scheme, however, lies in the way that such individual house types are knitted together through the orchestration of private, open space. The 'Borneo' area also accommodates a green belt, designed by De Architektengroep. Yet another building is designed by Enric Miralles. A curving pedestrian bridge, linking two other bridges, heightens the drama created by the building blocks themselves. These deliberate signature edifices impact upon the homogeneous structure of the low-rise units. Each of the three primary blocks claims its own communal courtyard.

The parameters set down by West 8 in the masterplan for housing were rigorous. Rather than losing the clear image of the existing harbour, where areas of storage space, dock and berth are differentiated through the normal bureaucratic welter of land-based planning dictats, West 8 took an alternative route. Coming as they did from a different, though related, discipline, as landscape architects they insisted upon the consolidation of what already existed. Thus they preserved the particular spatial land/water opposition of the built harbour, offering the latitude of extended shore or jetty frontages combined with functionally constructed promontories.

Borneo Sporenburg serves as a timely reminder that garden landscape also exists in the form of water landscape. This should be allowed to characterize the spatial definition and hierarchy of such spaces, rather than letting built form become dominant. One is reminded of Le Corbusier's late Venice Hospital project, essentially one comprising an interaction of water space with built space, with flickering light from the waters of the lagoon shimmering on the walls of the patients' rooms. Here he realized the spatial essence upon which Adriaan Geuze of West 8 has capitalized, the water space which defines the living space.

Geuze did not have in mind the historic imagery of harbour and portside, epitomized in 1950s England in the rigging, bollards and masts of a contrived waterside vernacular which then graced the pages of the *Architectural Review*. Geuze's inspiration, by contrast, was the geometric and volumetric massing of the contemporary container terminal. What Geuze focused upon was the subtle contrast, under the great, flat, Dutch sky, between the 'cosmic', limitless and yet reflective spatial expanses of water, and the essentially landlocked internal patios that characterize most of the housing. Geuze likewise recognized that for the inhabitants of the Netherlands nature is predominantly a reclaimed, man-made environment of polder landscape and ecology.

Inserted into this homogeneous scheme of waterside, low-rise housing blocks are the 'sculptural' blocks. These represent dramatic events, rather in the mode of deliberately discordant elements introduced, as by Stravinsky, into a repetitive harmony. The effect is energizing and creatively enriching.

Geuze realizes that in this man-made water landscape, such elemental factors as water reflection, sun angle, wind velocity and varying scents conspire to establish a variegated living environment which can establish the authenticity of the waterscape. In their masterplan, West 8 deliberately fostered the precedent of the double-fronted, Dutch canal house. The result is an animated but genuine street elevation

Above: The bridge that forms both a crossing point and a point of arrival, while linking the housing areas

Opposite: The water landscape is designed to permeate the individual apartments

system of great variety. It is in the manipulation of physical scale that the skills of the landscape architect are best expressed, with a special understanding of the rhythmic variation of macro- and micro-scale in existing and newly-created spaces. Borneo Sporenburg represents an elaboration on the scale of the minimal, medieval walled 'pleasaunce' (here epitomized by the patios). The idiom is further extended, becoming so great that it encompasses the horizon itself, but the view is contained artifically, bringing it within human reach in the constructed, waterside spaces. West 8 have become masters of this language, one so fundamental to landscape architecture. At Schiphol Airport (1997) they animated the dull expanses of cleared spaces by placing brightly-coloured floral plantings in swathes between the runways, replacing the traditional rides and avenues of formal and informal landscapes alike. In this way, rather than offering the sublime or the infinite, they offered visual tranquillizers for harassed travellers.

Here at Borneo Sporenburg, West 8 have given a new meaning to the specialization of landscape architect. Geuze has become the 'shaman' of the new environment, weaving a hitherto unrealized magic amongst the wharves and docks, animating the new habitats of inner-urban commuters with a twenty-first-century poetry. With Bernard Lassus and Martha Schwartz, Geuze has elevated landscape architecture to the realm of the master matrix or plan, whereby a creative master can raise environmental design to the level of the significant art of its period. The landscape architect today, as with Le Nôtre, or 'Capability' Brown, Jellicoe or Burle Marx in previous centuries, is truly fulfilled only when working within the living culture of his own period. The essence of garden landscape as defined in the past is transformed for the twenty-first century.

Garden Landscapes

Autoroute Rest Area
Nîmes–Caissargues, France, 1990

Bernard Lassus

Above: The landscape master plan, showing the separation of the Nîmes A54 autoroute and its conjunction with the planted picnic areas

Below: The Tour Magne, the landmark symbol that is visible from a distance on the autoroute Nîmes–Caissargues, and lit up at night

Bernard Lassus began his career as a painter and trained under Fernand Léger in Paris in the 1950s. This background has had an important influence upon his subsequent development as a landscape architect. Indeed, he would claim that art and landscape design are one and the same activity. He profoundly regrets the present division between the world of art and that of landscape architecture, and the extent to which this, in his opinion, represents a deficit in the educational balance that students have traditionally been obliged to recognize. However, Lassus has taken very positive steps to redress this situation. He laid the foundations as early as 1968 as Professor of Architecture at the École des Beaux Arts in Paris, and the fullest implementations of his philosophy took effect in the 1990s when he founded a Diploma of Advanced Studies in Landscape, jointly linking the École des Hautes Études with the École d'Architecture, Versailles.

One of the most original ground rules established by Lassus in his revision of landscape architecture concepts relates to a reduction of the status accorded to the 'natural' as opposed to the 'man-made' in environmental design. By this means, criteria become defined in relative terms rather than requiring the enforcement of absolutes. While this might at first seem potentially destructive of the natural environment, in reality it removes meaningless prohibitions and opens up the range of possibilities within which the landscape architect can extend the poetics of any given landscape in contemporary terms. He reduces the twentieth-century myths of heroic Modernism and its primacy of buildings over site. Of considerable contemporary value is the revalidation of ecological imperatives which may tend to override landscape values as such. In the twenty-first century such adjustments have been a necessary process in the swings of conventional wisdom as purveyed by conservative planners, conservation lobbyists and the enthusiasts for sustainability mandates.

The project Aire de Nîmes–Caissargues (Motorway Rest Area, Nîmes–Caissargues) lies on the extremely busy A54 autoroute. An existing service station was to be replaced when the scheme began in 1989. Giving the highest priority to landscaping such areas was an obvious step towards the mitigation of motorway stress and the provision of relief from the often dangerous, sometimes lethal, monotony of motor travel. Until the late 1990s, however, this was virtually unprecedented in Europe or the USA. Although these ends were clearly the primary objective for Lassus, he could also see the value of a degree of local interpretation. He thought it useful to provide a foretaste of, or perhaps an epigram to, a visit to the city of Nîmes. To rely on simulacrum could involve a descent into the worst kind of kitsch, but Lassus was fortunate in being able to import authentic ingredients from the city itself.

Lassus was able to bring to the site the neo-classical facade of the theatre at Nîmes, demolished in order to give adequate space to Norman Foster's superb Carré d'Art. The theatre itself had been part of a key ensemble of buildings inside Nîmes. Now this major fragment could be utilized to convey the essence of Nîmes to travellers. Lassus also created a pair of identical 'belvederes', mounted separately on higher ground nearby. These took the form of an ancient Roman relic, 'The Tour Magne', with the outline of the tower constructed in metal and lit up by night. By way of explanation as well as justification, a model of the original is exhibited within the metal enclosure. From this viewing position, reached by a spiral stair, the public are able to see the distant profile of Nîmes itself.

The rest area lies at an angle and runs under the autoroute like a green wedge, bordered continuously by symmetrically disposed avenues of trees along the 700 metres of its full extent. Lassus stipulated hackberry or nettle trees for the avenues, with freestanding groups of indigenous Provençal olive trees and cypresses. Cars park under the trees on the formal avenue, an extremely popular facility that satisfies a primitive need for shade, while also encouraging family picnics. Above all else, Lassus' intention as landscape architect is to represent people, to understand their instincts and inclinations and, as far as possible, to enable these natural and social aspirations to be fulfilled. It takes time to establish the trees, but the long-term benefits of such a solution are substantial in environmental and maintenance terms.

Bernard Lassus has developed the concept of the landscaped 'Aire de Repos' (rest-area) in various locally distinctive solutions in the period following Nîmes. Landscape designs for both the A83 Nantes–Niort autoroute and the A837 Saintes–Rochefort autoroute engaged quite distinctly with the local context. On the former, mainly timber structures were used for the Aire de Repos, and for the latter, metal structures. Lassus has worked to enhance or pick out certain existing landscape features. Such work is ongoing. Landscape architects have a vital task in relation to the motorway, with its landscape enhancement and its necessary rest areas. It is here that the poetics of landscape architecture may be seen, providing psychological balance and repose. Lassus has become a pioneer whose dreams are beginning to come to fruition for the benefit of society.

It would have been easy to review other landscape projects by Lassus, demonstrating his inherent ability to restore useful meaning to the theoretical discourse in landscape design. However, these projects connected with the transportation network in France reveal how only such a landscape philosophy can address the new age. Bernard Lassus has brought poetic inspiration to landscape architecture once more.

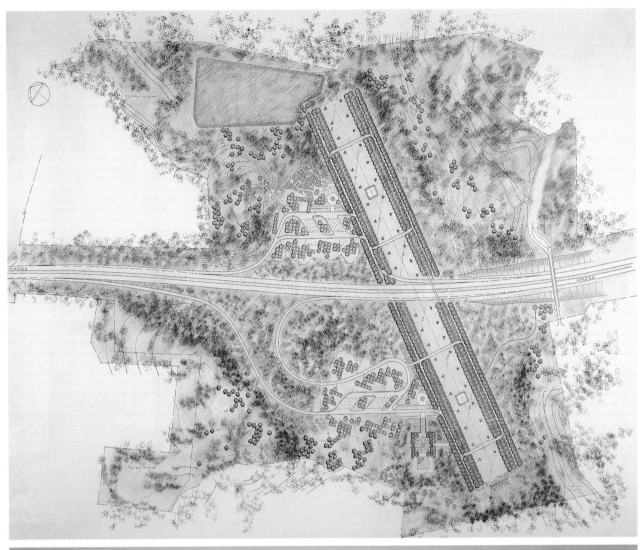

Right: The Nîmes theatre colonnade reflected in a pool

Below: The 700-metre long picnic area

Opposite, above: The re-erected neo-classical facade of the theatre from Nîmes, announcing the proximity of the city

Opposite, below: The pavilion for contemporary art

Urban Interventions

Never has the idea of interstitial spaces within the complex grain of cities seemed more essential than it does today. Cities continue to expand, and the range of human activity which city life sponsors grows apace. Cities contain our memorials, our shrines to religion, and are composed of networks of circulation, linking these with areas of commercial activity, stalls, discos, and embellished with the outdoor tables and chairs of cafeterias and restaurants. Pedestrian enclaves designed to link each neighbourhood to another must on the whole deny vehicular traffic.

Such primal models as Venice, with its superb hierarchy of great squares leading to tiny piazzas, Georgetown (Washington, DC) or Chelsea (London) provide inspiration today, yet are hard to emulate. Landscape architects are increasingly engaged in mediating between the historical memory contained in fragmentary enclaves, closes, stairs and passages, places of fleeting encounter, and urban furniture, utilizing new fountains, sculptures or playgrounds. Manhattan's Paley Park on East 53rd Street, with its gatehouses, tables and chairs, plus security guards, shows us what makes the Via Cassari in Palermo, Sicily, so European, with its proliferation of clothes lines, canopies and fruit stalls, and conversely Paley Park so American. Places like this characterize great cities as much as architectural monuments do.

In dealing with the activity of urban intervention, it is useful to have recourse to examples of revisionist thinking developed by two very different theorists over the past half-century: Gordon Cullen, on the one hand, and Colin Rowe on the other. Both transformed the manner in which cities are enhanced by significant intervention, opening up discourse and influencing practice as a result. The field each chose to recast had been largely frozen between functionality and dilettantism.[1]

Le Corbusier. La Ville Verte

Otto Wagner, Zedlitzhalle, Vienna (second design, 1933). Two identical entrances dominate the central site of intervention in this design for an Arts and Crafts exhibition hall

Accidents which Engage Concepts

Such interstices also happen when differing city grids collide: these are the left-over edge spaces, offering special opportunities for the creation of identity at a human scale.

Colin Rowe was timely in his wholesale demolition of the 'cult of English villages, Italian hill towns, and North African casbahs, [that] was above all else a matter of felicitous happenings and anonymous architecture.'[2] In the 1960s the key issue was whether this ideal of townscape, propagated by Cullen, could be made more palliative by way of being 'affiliated to Cubist and post-Cubist tradition'. Townscape bore witness, it seems, to a highly interesting theory of 'the accident'. Rowe, perceptively as well as provocatively, then offered that the model was surely Serlio's popular and Comic Scene rather than the aristocratic and Tragic Scene which Utopia had consistently employed. In practice, however, townscape seems to have lacked any ideal referent for the engaging 'accidents' that it sought to promote. As a result, its tendency has been to provide sensation without

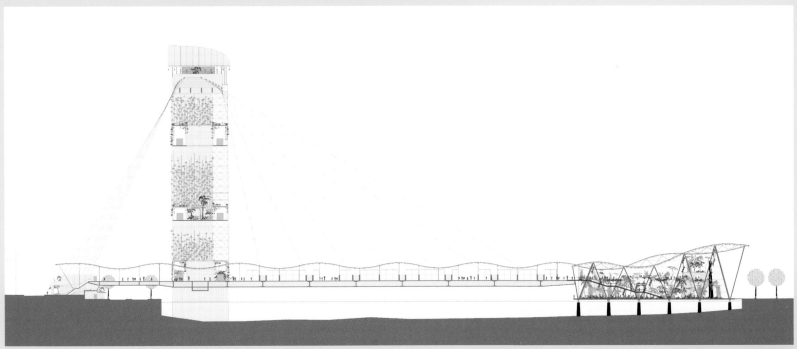

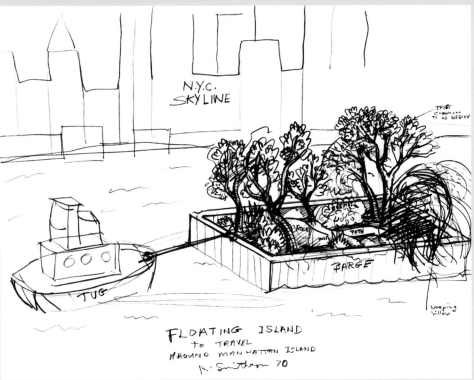

Antoine Grumbach, longitudinal section of the Garden Bridge, competition entry for the River Thames crossing, exhibited at 'Living Bridges', Royal Academy, London, September (1986)

Robert Smithson, Study for Floating Island to Travel Around Manhattan Island (1970), pencil on paper. A brilliant visual metaphor encapsulating the problem of 'greening the city'

plan, to appeal to the eye and not to the mind, and, while usefully sponsoring a perceptual world, to devalue a world of concepts.

In his elaboration of the theory that the garden is a critique of the city, Colin Rowe developed an intriguing comparison between the regularity of Versailles and the disorganized curiosity of the Villa Adriana at Tivoli. Over the past decade a new generation has become involved in the garden debate, which had apparently reached deadlock. The new contributors recognize the primary role of hard and soft landscaping in enabling and facilitating a new perceptual, as well as purely conceptual, basis for urban interventions.

This selection of urban interventions includes Juhani Pallasmaa's small-scale but highly charged transitional node within highly active city-centre pedestrian routes: a place to pause momentarily in the flux; and Ninebark's elegant and moving contemporary interpretation of the monumental and local. Mikyoung Kim has revealed in the Moylan school playground how urban ingredients provide surprise, privacy and crossover and can also enhance group activity.

Colin Rowe, Axonometric: Peter Carl, Judith di Maio, Steven Peterson and Colin Rowe. The Circo Massimo, the Palatino, the Celio and the Colosseum (1978), from *Roma Interotta*, edited by Jennifer Franchina (Rome) 1979. The team ingeniously articulated various landscape elements within what Rowe described as 'the most ancient Roman debris', providing a loose organizing template set against the fragmented nature of the city

Nodalities

The missing element in the enrichment of the twentieth-century city was always landscaping. In seventeenth-century Rome, one coded interstitial form of punctuation to be developed from the classical repertoire was the obelisk. At the Porto del Popolo, adjacent to the Church of Santa Maria del Popolo, Pope Sixtus V interposed just such a symbol, which incidentally enhanced a much older fountain there. Such nodalities inevitably interconnect across a city. In the late twentieth century it was anticipated that a contemporary equivalent would be the growing prevalence of urban sculpture, whether figurative or abstract.

The recognition of existing resources is a fundamental necessity for the landscapist working within the urban context. Antoine Grumbach, the French urban designer, was almost alone in recognizing the idea of a 'vegetal archaeology'. This was developed in his entry for the famous 1978 Roma Interrotta competition.[3] He described this phenomenon as a 'form of parasitic vegetation which accompanies the limits between public and private domains, reveals the existence of a continuous vegetal formation whose solutions are innumerable.' Grumbach continued, 'never catalogued, never classified, this continuous presence of vegetation becomes by the very fact that we can see it, a cultural object essential to the nature of urban structure … in ancient Rome whether sixteenth-century or in the present, what it bears witness to is the everlasting trace of a relationship between the city and nature.'

In his Parque en Lancy on the edge of Geneva, Georges Descombes, albeit in a less central intervention, also reverts to this vegetal archaeology, where he reconciles both natural and artificial realities, using elements which 'establish a connection between the individual and the essence of a place'. For example, there is a main pathway through a complex and somewhat transitional site. In the smallest detail Descombes' philosophy in this respect becomes evident: where the path bisects the root system of trees, the roots remain partially exposed, but not cut, nor covered over.

Pioneers of the Genius Loci

The townplanner Gordon Cullen was right to complain in 1971 of being misunderstood by architects who, in their uninspired reliance on cobbles and bollards to signify the vernacular, were to parody his work. What Cullen really conveyed in his important text of the time was the importance of materiality and texture in urban interventions. Cullen's early townscape studies for Westminster clarify the integrity and originality of his thinking. Cullen had collaborated with the designer Eric de Maré as early as 1949 on a proposal for a Thames linear park. He was also alone at the time in seeking to explore the role of trees with architecture. But what he unequivocally established was the extent to which pedestrianized cities required a frequent intervention through the presentation of numerous spatially structured events. 'Serial vision' as conceived by Cullen was seen to apply to all sequential movement in cities. His development of a viable system of notation (1968) appeared to break new ground in establishing a referent system, but opportunities for its implementation and testing were not to occur, despite its value as an analytical tool, purpose-made to assist the process of intervention.[4]

Like Antoine Grumbach, Colin Rowe had entered the Roma Interrotta competition in 1978. Rowe had entered with an inspired group of former students.[5] Their entry significantly offered one important landscape intervention, whereby a late nineteenth-century bridge of no great significance, the Viadotto Margherita, connecting the gardens of the former Villa Albani with the Piazzale dell'Aventino, became 'indispensable'. Within the overall context of an Arcadian valley, 'densely enclosed by a framework of pines, palms, oleanders and rhododendrons', occurred to Rowe 'perhaps the most seductive of all Roman celebrations of water, the Circus Maximus…' In his publication *Collage City* (with Fred Koetter), Rowe emphasized the importance of a number of such key interventions. For example, the 'stabilizer' space, as such, was one of a series of 'magically useless points or navels' which nonetheless essentially exhibited a coherent geometry. 'Splendid public terraces', commanding sometimes landscape, sometimes water features, were to be exemplary interventions. Rowe also considered as useful various 'nostalgia-producing instruments', 'scientific of the future' yet also 'romantic of the past'. Rowe was elsewhere to say that 'the potential of the garden, what it should suggest to the planner … continues to be very little noticed.'[6]

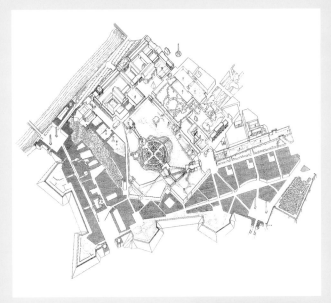

Plan: Peter Carl, Judith di Maio, Steven Peterson and Colin Rowe. The Aventino and Orto Botanico (1978), from *Roma Interrotta*, edited by Jennifer Franchina (Rome) 1979

Links which Redefine City-Space

Bridges have traditionally conveyed their infrastructural importance by transcending the purely technical. When the bridge becomes non-vehicular, typically operating as a pedestrian conduit, drama and perspective result from the river crossing, and frequently dramatic perspectives are unexpectedly disclosed. The concept by Antoine Grumbach of a 'Garden Bridge' in a competition for the Thames was an inspiring fusion of garden elements with engineering.[7] Latterly, Norman Foster's Millennium Bridge, jointly executed and finally perfected with Arup, has opened up St Paul's Cathedral to the river and Tate Modern. The precedent always existed: in the opening decade of the twentieth century, Otto Wagner in Vienna was to create meticulous combinations of masonry and steelwork. The Zeile bridge, and that over the Dublinger Hauptstrasse, triumphally wedded design aesthetic and engineering, creating major new monuments by such interventions in core areas of Vienna. In the new century, the Gateshead Millennium Bridge, by Wilkinson and Eyre, linking that community with Newcastle across the River Tyne, has transformed both sides of the river in a city with an existing plethora of historic crossings.

Such urban interventions today seek increasingly to remedy the deficit of the immediate past. 'Vegetation' and planting too can transform and catalyse routes, as do the smaller spaces and crossings, operating as coded symbols. The revisions of the early propagandists such as Rowe in America and Cullen in Europe took decades to be truly assimilated, and persistent efforts in the few competitions at this time generally failed to produce success for new ideas about intervention.

Scale and Sanctuary

Amongst the newer landscape practitioners, the Edinburgh-based group Gross Max examines each project context to find the inherent characteristic of the place; and so seeks initially to isolate such special historical factors and incidentals as can be traced, to establish a greatly enhanced entity. A small body of newer landscape architects are working in this manner, where a holistic, exclusively architectural approach invariably seems deficient. On a much greater scale, Hargreaves at Homebush, the park for the Sydney Olympic Games (2000) had to 'intervene' in a massively-scaled esplanade, where the overwhelming scale of the stadia reduced human scale at pedestrian level to the diminutive. The Sydney firm of architects Tonkin Zulaikha Greer developed an effective design for urban street furniture, such as lights, signing and seating. This transformed the windy, hard-landscaped 'prairie' between the buildings. In addition, water features and a combination of garden and wilder planting was installed at key points, maintaining a natural ecology for an area that was otherwise seriously at risk. Homebush stands as a successful example of interdisciplinary collaboration, but the controlling reach of the landscape architects was always critical.

There is a growing need for multi-disciplinary teams in the realm of urban

Giambattista Piranesi, 'Ancient Circus of Mars with neighbouring Monuments viewed from the Via Appia', Frontispiece of *Le Antichità Romane III* (1756)

intervention. Land artists, installation artists and sculptors of all persuasions have a role. These creative collaborations work best when all the different practitioners are involved with the landscape brief from the outset, rather than being called in as late additions.

The interpretation of the modern landscape is a vital activity which seems to be best exercised by the artist in the developing role of documentary photographer and plotter of the essence of place. Outdoor space cannot be 'reinvented', since it has always existed within our minds; however it can certainly benefit from reinterpretation. Such transformations can also be envisaged as interventions that redefine the value of urbanity, incorporating the semblance of risk into otherwise bland, urban surroundings. It can be readily observed that a momentum has grown over the past two generations that has been initiated by relatively few thinkers. Such theorists as Kevin Lynch and Jane Jacobs laid down the social criteria that formed the urban context of design innovation expressed by Cullen and Grumbach. Colin Rowe was able to acknowledge the new interest in landscape; and yet only today can such innovative speculation at last be realized, as opposed to confined within competition documents to sink without trace.

Notes

1 See David Gosling, *Gordon Cullen: Visions of Urban Design*, London: Academy Editions, 1996, p.8. Cullen justifiably claimed (as in his Introduction to *The Concise Townscape*, 1971) that architects and planners had 'completely misunderstood his message with their banal use of cobbles and bollards'

2 Colin Rowe and Fred Koettler, *Collage City*, Cambridge, MA: MIT Press, 1978, pp.36 and 88

3 *Roma Interotta*, Rome: Incontri Internazionali d'Arte and Officina Edizioni, 1979, pp.65–81. Grumbach's own scheme ('A Challenge to Architecture') includes transformations with 'vegetation' and planting. Grumbach develops here the concept of 'vegetal archaeology, the form of "parasitic" vegetation occupying the limits between private and public domains.'

4 'Excursus', *Collage City, op. cit.*, pp.151–73

5 *Roma Interotta, op. cit.*, pp. 136–58

6 Ibid., p.175

7 See 'Antoine Grumbach – The Garden Bridge', competition entry, in Peter Murray and Mary Anne Stevens (eds.), *Living Bridges: The Inhabited Bridge, Past, Present and Future*, London: Prestel Ltd, 1996, pp.140–3

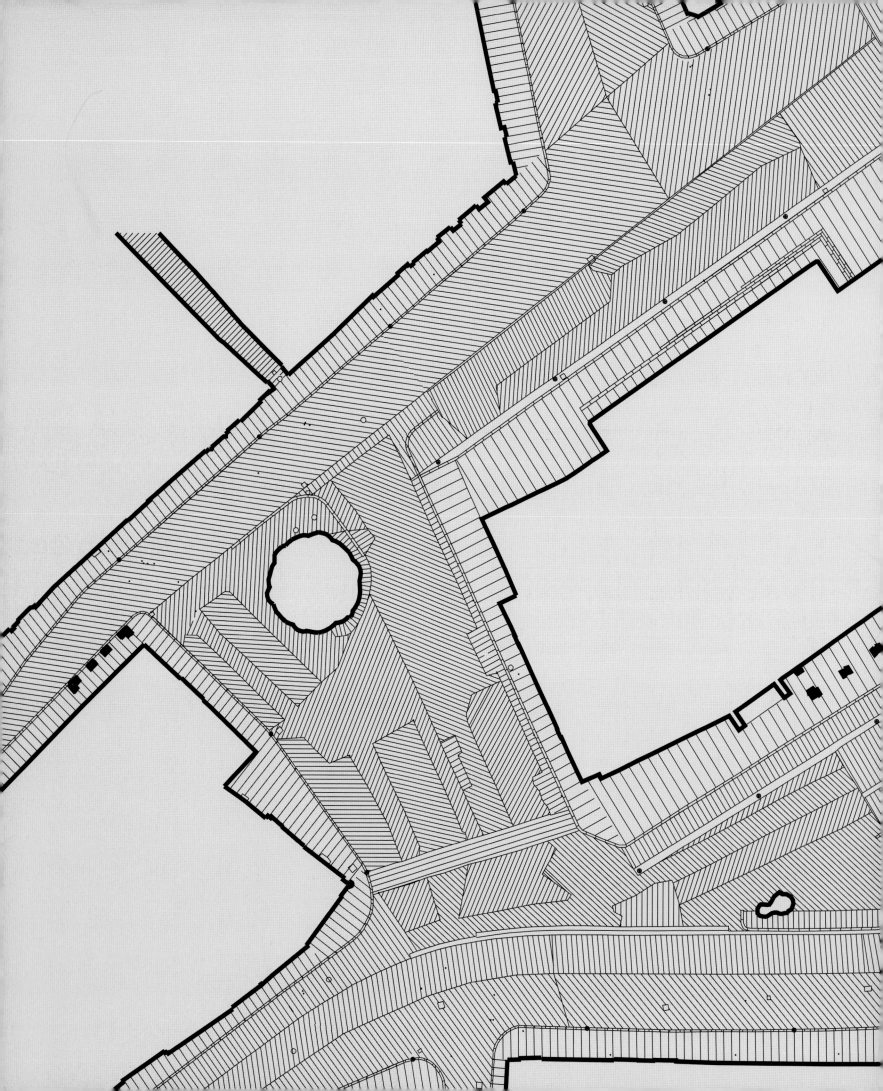

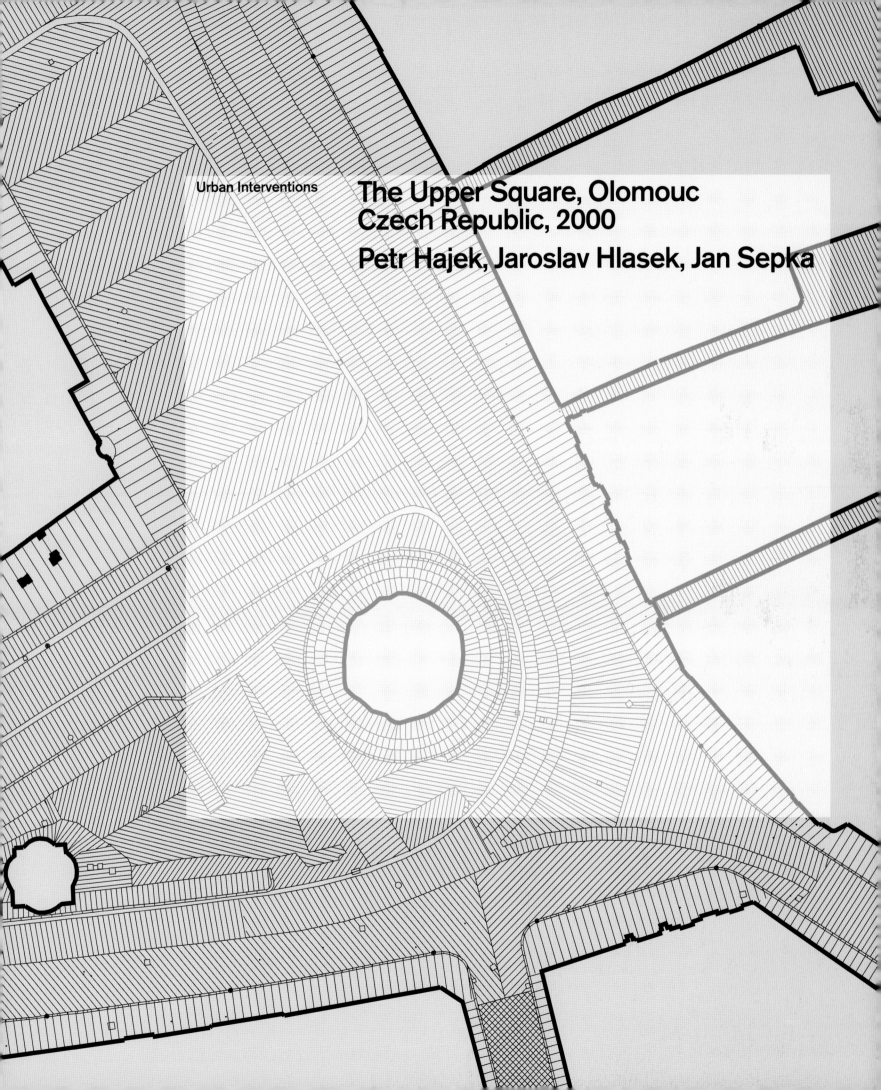

Urban Interventions

The Upper Square, Olomouc
Czech Republic, 2000
Petr Hajek, Jaroslav Hlasek, Jan Sepka

Far right: Overview of the Upper Square in context with important historic monuments in the historic core of Olomouc

The city of Olomouc lies within the Czech Republic. It formed a convenient stopping place on the old route from Prague, the capital, to the Polish city of Krakow, across the Polish border. This endowed it with significant status in its own right. Indeed, until 1640 Olmutz, as it was known in German, was the capital of the province of Moravia. Both the seat of a bishopric, and a university founded in 1573 (subsequently reduced to a theological faculty), the fifteenth-century Gothic cathedral and town hall stand witness to a long and civilized heritage. Franz von Dietrichstein, born in Spain, was typical of the worldly holders of the early seventeenth-century bishopric.

The square at the centre is described today by the architects as 'a parlour with a town hall set in the middle, with fountains and a patched up carpet on the floor.' This conveys the somewhat threadbare survival of the historic fabric of the square. But the great expanse of this superb urban space in fact on an average day puts one more in mind of the ornately impressive spatial disposition of one of the Czech Republic's great libraries, such as the magnificent eighteenth-century monastery library at Vyssi Brod (Hohenfurth), with its dramatic ceiling painting which conveys a sense of spatial uplift; or else the hall of the University Library at Clementinum in Prague itself (c.1722). This sense of a massive, externalized chamber is prevalent in the Upper Square at Olomouc still. Likewise, the ornately topped facades of the library stacks convey both individuality and a collective harmony, which is equally evident here, where the surrounding buildings stand.

The designers of the renovations to the square have had the good fortune to work on a square where, ironically due to the austerity and control of the period of communist government of Czechoslovakia, commercial intrusion and erosion of this great space was virtually non-existent. In 1946 Olomouc University was re-established, and the city fathers sought to recover an appropriate solemnity for this administrative, episcopal and intellectual core of the city's existence, which has a population of some 80,000 today.

The so-called 'patched-up carpet' of the square clearly formed a key priority in this process of recovery: rather than focussing on the surrounding buildings, it was the hard landscaping that was rightly seen to be the key to a new spirit for the square. A 'carpet' thus spread across the entire surface of the square at one level, allows the kerbs and pavements to remain, but levelled out as a consistent surface. Its original compositon of pavings, which includes deliberately directional lines across, was maintained with careful repairs where necessary.

Brass strips, like a golden ribbon, frame all the separate areas of the pavings and so continue the emphasis on the directional and historic pedestrian flows, a modern artefact installed, but one which complements the existing spatial topology. The collage of varied pavings is thus linked together effectively rather than offering a fragmented set of memories. Variously, two-point focal perspectives linking the key seventeenth- and eighteenth-century buildings are reinforced.

Lighting has formed a special study: the designers have sought to integrate two circles of street lighting which particularly emphasise the Upper Square at night or in winter dusk, using indirect light which provides an even distribution of light across the entire square surface. Then the second, complementary circle of lights is run round the central town hall, thus gently illuminating the spaces between the fountains, monuments, circles and arcades. Separate illuminations then pick out key monuments or objects in space, including a bronze relief model of the centre of Olomouc. The concept for the Upper Square provides a stable light intensity which does not clash with the directional pools of light over the objects.

Street furniture has formed another critical priority here. The designers say this completes the image of the square as a parlour; but it is more than this. Admittedly these furniture elements combine to create almost an interior quality. Not only the lamps, but benches (in much demand), a stand for bicycles, and litter bins, are all exemplary items of industrial design. The concept of urban *arredamento* is demonstrated to perfection. And on the actual surfaces of the so-called 'carpet', details such as sewer inlets, which are usually ignored, have been specially cast and installed into the pavings. Even the ubiquitous parking meters and tourist information boards are incorporated without compromising the historic grain of the square.

At Olomouc can be observed an attention to design detail which emulates undoubtedly both the concerns of Dimitri Pikionis (at the Acropolis, Athens) and also the earlier ingenuity of Jan Plecnik in Slovenia and in Prague itself. What is interesting is that Daniel Libeskind and Lutzow 7, in the spaces around the Jewish Museum, Berlin (see page 146), and indeed Gross Max, as well as Juhani Pallasmaa at Helsinki, in their own urban interventions reveal, without dramatizing the context, this ongoing tradition of hard landscape design perfectionism. But Olomouc remains an outstanding example, a model for all designers concerned with the adaptation of the urban 'room'. The concept of urban intervention as room, offering the public equivalent of the private domestic space, or *salone*, is a longstanding urban provision too readily forgotten in the realm of shopping malls and consumer temples. Here the true key to success has derived from the immaculate detailing. The result is in a class of its own for the present.

Far right: View over Upper Square and baroque fountain: this gives the overall sense of harmony with surrounding contemporary elements, such as seating, lighting, manholes, all set within the hard urban landscaping of the pavings and divisions, the 'carpet' so important to the architects

Examples of specially designed street furniture

Above left: Bicycle racks

Above right: Manhole inset

Below left: Monuments preserved

Below right: Seating and lighting installation

Urban Interventions

**Aleksanderinkatu
Helsinki, Finland, 1993**

Juhani Pallasmaa

The re-entrant facing three of the five 'obelisks'. In the spring the street is filled with pedestrians and users of the street bar and tables

The retrieval of city spaces from obscurity is a critical task for the urban designer, architect or landscape architect. Aleksanderinkatu 15 was completed in 1991, and forms an essential part of the revived pedestrian network of central Helsinki. In this city of climatic extremes which are often aggravated by the wind effect from high blocks, which sends leaves, paper or plastic shopping bags and discarded food containers swirling across the paths of unsuspecting walkers, a forgotten courtyard can become hazardous in many ways. At the same time, very small spaces in the city, if intelligently considered, can provide sanctuary in summer and shelter in winter.

Juhani Pallasmaa has been particularly intrigued by making this project for a small urban space. As he says himself:

I confront the city with my body: my legs measure the length of the arcade and the width of the square; my gaze unconsciously projects my body onto the facade of the cathedral where it roams over the mouldings and contours, sensing the size of recesses and projections ... I experience myself in the city, and the city exists through my embodied experience. The city and my body supplement and define each other.

Pallasmaa considers the human body to be the centre of the experiential world. He also reminds us how the cities of film-makers, built up of momentary fragments, envelop us with the full vigour of fragments of real cities. 'The streets in great paintings continue around street corners and past the edges of the picture frame into the invisible with all the intricacies of life.'[1] Pallasmaa's space here has all the characteristics of such an enigmatic painting. Landscaping is about colour and texture, scale, gradation and diminishing perspective, especially within such a frame of surrounding buildings. As, for example, in the paintings of De Chirico, mysteries of coincidental windows, open and closed, of dramatic changes in tonality, cannot always be explained. Here at Aleksanderinkatu, Pallasmaa provides a rendezvous for the mind.

Pallasmaa had no wish to make the passage and small courtyard into an enclosed interior space. His inspiration for the design of the courtyard was drawn from the memorable lanes and backyards common in southern climates. Collage has also been used as a method of composing the

aggregated surfaces and planes, together with the vertical columns in differing materials and finishes that allow spatial penetration. Various visual and tactile, seemingly random, events occur and are strongly perceptible as one walks through, bringing a sense of discontinuity in contrast to the momentum of the passage. Pallasmaa's choice of colour is reminiscent of Mexican towns and villages. The variations simply adjust to the scale of the courtyard and mediate natural light effects. The south wall has been deliberately rendered in 'warm' tones while the north wall, which is lighter and catches spring and summer sun more readily, is rendered in 'colder' colours. The courtyard building is blue-green, and is covered with a net for climbing plants. Two curves of black and red granite sets intersect at ground level; these also visually connect as pavement with the three established points of entry to the space. A white marble disc, positioned in the centre of this concentric paving plan, signifies the centre unequivocally in such an active space.

At the end of the courtyard a trio of freestanding sculptural columns, a kind of Minimalist colonnade, is characterized by three separate sections: one column is circular and in timber; the second is triangular and made of stainless steel; and the third is in black granite, and square. In his earlier art museum for the northern city of Rovaniemi (1986), Pallasmaa enhanced the importance of the entrance in a similarly Minimalist way with five tall granite columns, also freestanding on the exterior, contributing to the complex image of the museum and abandoning the precepts of a single mind. Pallasmaa believes that collage as such is 'the most appropriate medium for illustrating this reality'. Here at Aleksanderinkatu this is certainly evident. The function of these columns is clearly a psychological one; but it also marks the line between the areas reserved for pedestrians and vehicles. The subtle, tactile combination of form and material here orchestrated by Pallasmaa distracts one's attention from the grim scale of the upper parts of the courtyard, beyond the designer's reach and control. Heavy, glazed roof structures are visually 'weighted' in order to develop the impression of verticality here, as well as intervening against the space's depressing upper reaches. As well as protecting the courtyard from the flurries of winter snow, the oblique lines employed in the design bring a sense of movement to an otherwise static space.

Right: Initial sketch concept for
the installation of the 'well' and
bronze spout as a city
'fragment'

Far right: Conceptual sketch for
an oriel window overlooking the
ground level

Below: Ground plan showing
the three pedestrian routes by
which the space is entered, the
three 'obelisks' (below left), and
the concentric pavings

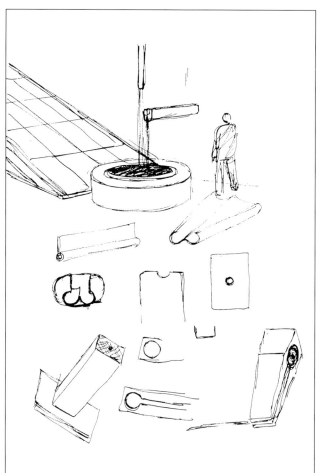

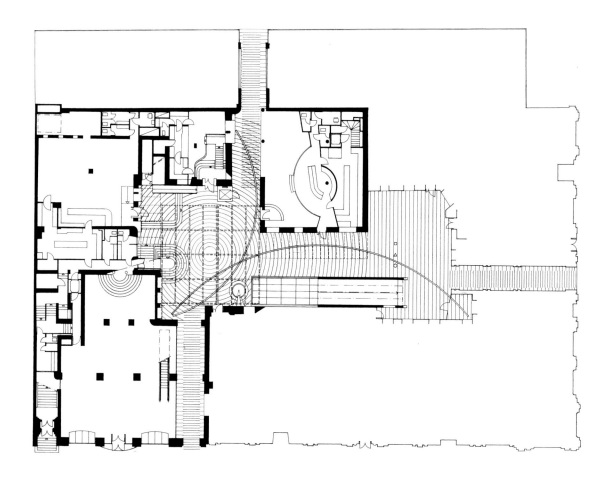

Right: The reflective and
material qualities of the three
'obelisks'

Far right: The interaction of
concentric steps and pavings

Sound is also important, both present and absent.
Pallasmaa draws our attention to Kakuzo Okakura's *The
Book of Tea*:

> Nothing breaks the silence save the note of the boiling
> water in the iron kettle. The kettle sings well, for pieces of
> iron are so arranged in the bottom as to produce a
> peculiar melody in which one may hear the echoes of a
> cataract muffled by clouds, of a distant sea breaking
> among the rocks, a rainstorm sweeping through a bamboo
> forest, or of the swaying of pines on some faraway hill.

Here, rainwater running along the various gutters
and drainpipes allows a varying sound experience and finally
sinks into a village 'well', which supplies water even in dry
weather through a bronze spout; but this can also freeze,
allowing other sounds to prevail in the muffled regime of
winter. Even in the midst of the city, Pallasmaa has turned
everyday experience into something magical.

This small Helsinki scheme, not even a *piazzetta* in
scale, summarizes the urban landscape potential of a
contemporary application of collage and Minimalist thinking,
in line with contemporary developments in the visual arts.
Landscape architects have long been inspired by Land and
Installation artists and here, in an utterly depressing and
confined space, the architect has been able to combine an
awareness of contemporary issues in art with magic and
alchemy, converting negative into positive place-form.

1   Teemu Taskinen of the Pallasmaa office, project description, 1991

Whiteinch Cross
Glasgow, UK, 1999

Gross Max

Gross Max's drawn overview, showing the correlation of all elements

Gross Max is a group of three European landscape designers who have established themselves in Edinburgh, although they operate in a wholly international context. Bridget Baines, Eelco Hooftman and Ross Ballard have made their reputation through a series of dramatic competition entries in Britain and across Europe. Through their designs they have successfully gained an avant-garde prominence, mostly for significant interventions within the hard urban grain of various cities. The first scheme they executed, however, was in the remote Shetland Islands. Hooftman in particular brought a fresh eye to Scotland, and to the problems of the landscape profession in Britain. As early as 1993, Eelco Hooftman wrote that 'the urban fringe, the expansion joint between town and countryside, has become a commercial *intifada* of *ad hoc* consumerism, and meanwhile our cities are turned inside out. Everlasting greenbelt is transformed overnight into exploding technicolour – goldbelts full of business opportunities, redbelts of Wimpey housing estates and blackbelts of parking tarmac.'[2] Gross Max have since then single-mindedly proposed a series of masterly interventions within London, at St Johns Square in Clerkenwell, Hackney Town Hall and Lyric Square, Hammersmith. They have also worked on the City Gardens project in Rotterdam. Collaboration with different artists has become normal in these developments.

Whiteinch Cross was commissioned by Glasgow's UK City of Architecture and Design programme 1999, directed by Deyan Sudjic. This central site had become derelict and redundant. It had, within living memory, been a place for watering horses. Gross Max accordingly evolved the design of a wall of water flowing gently across some 8 metres (26 feet), over sheets of Cor-Ten steel, thus also incorporating the memory of past shipbuilding nearby. The artist Adam Barker-Mill was engaged to make a 12-metre (40-foot) white tower, internally a translucent blue that varies in intensity according to the time of day or night. In contrast, the ground-level is paved with Clashach sandstone streaked with iron deposit. The square is divided into two level platforms and articulated with two substantial freestanding walls in conjunction with a transparent pergola construction in galvanized steel. Trees have been both preserved (in protective cast-iron grilles) and reintroduced to emphasize the sanctuary offered by the site against the bustle of city life. Seats which each accommodate one or – at a pinch – two people, nestle in their shade, and the walls provide a buffer against the traffic noise from the adjacent street.

What had been an abandoned, flyblown patch with threadbare trees has in this way been transformed into an important urban experience for the passer-by. This, too, is a natural reminder, even a commemoration by light and shade, of the reality of site and city past.

From this radical urban debut, Gross Max have moved on to consider Hackney Town Hall, London, where an active period of local consultation has led to a scheme that fully vindicates the process of public discussion. The Town Hall is itself a listed Art-Deco building (1934–7), and local feeling favoured the re-establishment of the typical 'green retreat'. This concept of sanctuary has been extended through a cohesion of water and light, in a space dominated by two massive flower beds, also listed. Gross Max simply incorporated and re-presented these low-slung monuments to posterity, substituting water pools for the ageing flower beds. To reintroduce colour and planted form, they added flowering trees, which better enhance the substantial scale, while preserving the place-form of the listed beds intact.

At St John's Square, London, a canopy of light will be achieved using high lamp-posts topped with horizontal glass squares. The Lyric, Hammersmith project, London, and a scheme for the Bullring, Birmingham both testify to the way in which Gross Max bear the future in mind, without abandoning the past. They have grasped an old *métier* for urban intervention by landscape architects, usually on the margins, and they take centre stage, making their name stick in the grist of urban planning, ensuring that landscape design features earlier within a protracted process previously monopolized by architects and town planners. (Witness the disaster of William Holford's postwar Paternoster Square.)

Gross Max are not simply present as technicians or jobbing artists in the old landscapist mode, but as philosopher-designers with a fundamental quest to reinvent the nature of city space itself. The mnemonic nature of urbanity, the qualities of intimacy and the necessary authenticities of the historical frame have been recovered. Bridget Baines of Gross Max says: 'Cities are rediscovering themselves. It's almost like medieval times, they want to be special. It's all about city identity – and the landscape architect can help to provide that. Not in a nostalgic but in a forward-looking way.'[3] Gross Max also strive to create for cities a 'Pandora's box of full of metropolitan sensual delights'.[4] In their work for Expo 2000 at Hanover, they demonstrated their breadth of vision in a temporary exhibition context where a considerable tract of the site was

still a cornfield. This they retained as an *objet trouvé*, along with the lonely farmer on his combine-harvester who became a hedonistic hero of Expo 2000, his harvest and his subsequent ploughing becoming an important part of the show. As in the hands of an artist, it is not so much the existence of an unexpected event but the potential to develop it that is the role of the designer.

Eelco propounds the concept of the 'avant garden', peopled with artists, architects and designers. 'I am happy to remain a designer – I work with artists but I don't want to become one myself.'[5] At Hackney, Gross Max invited a composer, Matt Rogalsky, to make a 'soundscape' to be activated by those walking across the square, and computerized underwater lights in the ponds that will rhythmically change hue.

In garden history, there was always the *mise-en-scène*. Gross Max have managed to update this convincingly for the twenty-first century. Whether designing a contemporary medical garden in the tradition of the *hortus conclusus* on an inner urban site, as they did for Glasgow University, or an updated 'Lustgarten' in Berlin's Potsdamer Platz, Gross Max have convincingly proved that landscape design intervening in cities demands 'a change of scenery'.[6]

2 Eelco Hooftman, 'Landscape off its Trolley', *Sunday Times* (Scotland), 14 Nov 1993, p.11
3 Ibid.
4 Michael Spens, interview with Bridget Baines, Gross Max office, Edinburgh, April 2002
5 Michael Spens, interview with Eelco Hooftman, Gross Max office, Edinburgh, April 2002
6 Eelco Hooftman, Gross Max brochure, April 2002, p.1: 'A change of scenery: why suffocate on an overdose of chlorophyll if we can boost our level of adrenaline instead ... The optimism of Gross Max Landscape Architects acts as a refreshing breeze in the conservative establishment of British landscape architecture.'

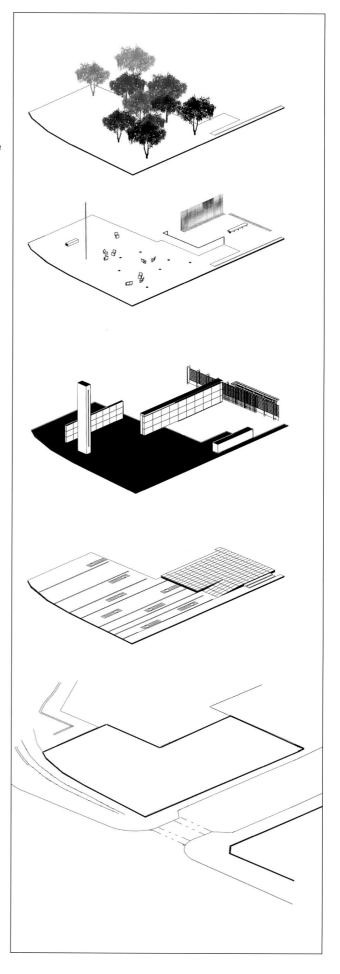

Opposite: Exploded diagram of the key elements of the project: trees, incidental seating, walls, sculptured tower, pavings and site

Above: Whiteinch Cross, illumination by night. Twenty-four-hour activation is a characteristic of Gross Max's urban landscaping

Right: The concept of oasis, sanctuary in the city – seats, trees, sun and shade

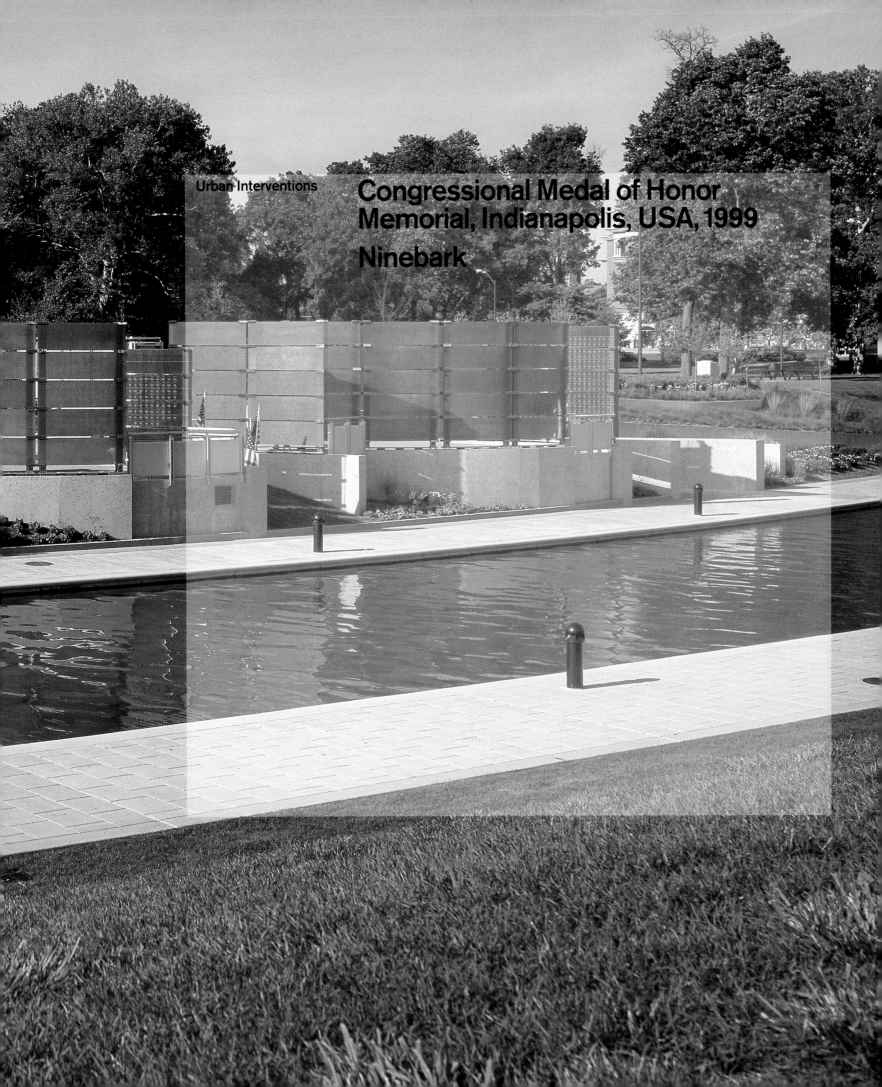

Urban Interventions

Congressional Medal of Honor Memorial, Indianapolis, USA, 1999

Ninebark

Above: Overview of the memorial site at the eastern end of the central canal and walkways

Below left: The curved glass panels in detail

Below right: The Indianapolis skyline and the illuminated memorial by night

War impacts on the civilian life of cities through the crude, mechanical force of bombs and missiles. Elsewhere reference has been made to the outstanding Gallipoli Museum, Turkey, which choreographs a tragic history of massive and unnecessary deaths. But Indianapolis hosts a different kind of commemoration, for 3,433 heroic male and female recipients of the Congressional Medal of Honor; nor does this memorial seek in any way to glorify war but rather to form a tribute to the spirit of humanity, where acts of personal self-sacrifice are witness to a greater cause. Above all else, a sense of place becomes a prerequisite. An awareness, perhaps, of the contrasting powers of light and darkness has to be brought to bear.

The site is urban, in a central location at the eastern end of Indianapolis' central canal. The slope selected was some 15 metres (16 yards) wide and 260 metres (283 yards) long, with a level change downwards of some 4 metres (13 feet) from the upper, treebound edge to the canal itself.

The memorial was conceived by Eric Fulford and Ann Reed of Ninebark Inc, beginning as a series of sails, 27 in number. Curved concrete walls of 'conflict' tear across the green slope, disrupting the normal continuum of walking and jogging. The sails are constructed in glass, upon which are engraved the names of all who have so distinguished themselves. Many recipients were citizens rather than regular service personnel, torn from their routine lives across the US, now to 'sail' together. A few are still alive today. Each of the two main arcs of sails represents part of distinctive conflicts, as far back as the Civil War. Nor is the memorial finite, any more than wars will ever cease, and it continues to accommodate names. Ominous blank sails therefore float too, as yet unmarked by the names of the future. Notably, there is also a peacekeepers' sail reserved in the armada for those who have earned the Congressional Medal on peacekeeping engagements – it is already engraved with three names.

Eric Fulford trained in Urban Design and Countryside Planning at Edinburgh University, and Ann Reed is a graduate of Texas A & M University. Experience from widely differing locations has evidently been successfully pooled for such a collaborative venture. The planting is discreet and harmoniously constrained, with lawns and some mixed planting and varied grasses. A wide walkway marks the canal edge.

Fulford's initial training was in geology, and he was subsequently a Rome Prize Fellow. He is remembered in Rome for a remarkably detailed 360-degree drawing of the Campo de' Fiori, which took seven months to execute. This attention to detail was invaluable for the design of the memorial's jointing and fixing systems, much of which was innovative. A Marine veteran who happened to be a retired glazier was happy to be 're-enlisted' to manage the complex installation and setting up of the glass panels.

Viewed from afar, the sails seem to move like a flotilla in the wind, grouped together yet sailing individually. Clearly any heavier material, however reflective, would lack the essential transparency, light-responsiveness and fluidity of the light-refracting glass. As appropriate to a memorial to the highest human endeavour, there are pools of light and remarkably few shadows. Light, sound and wind can collude here in the core of the city, playing upon the individual and collective memories of visitors. Eric Fulford says: 'We imagined the sound of the stories echoing over the rustling grass and blowing wind of the landscape.'[7]

The recorded voices of the survivors of conflicts are linked to a computerized system of lights. These are activated to gently illuminate particular sails and the names on them at any given time. A significant grouping of mature trees along the upper edge of the site is a great bonus, creating the only shadows on the site.

Materiality and spirituality are somehow linked together: Fulford himself produced a massive volume of necessary constructional details, rather than lose control to an intermediate detailer. The fixings and dimensions of the sails were complicated by the choice of glass. 'Glass is a living material,' says Fulford, 'and light moves and affects the glass in a variety of ways.'[8] The material nature of the glass is complemented by tactility, as visitors are encouraged to touch the names etched on the front of each sail. On the back, and out of reach, details of the service given by the individual are etched into the glass together, where appropriate, with the active location of the event. On this side

Right: Fulford and Reed have manipulated the reflective quality of the translucent glass screens in the context of the waterside walkways, set against the towers of the central business district

Opposite, above: The transition from the memorial panels to the planted landscaping surround

Opposite, below: The glass panels are skilfully manipulated on different levels

too, abstract imagery of events and places is etched, such as fields, plants, earth and stars. The glass panels are curved, with front and back clearly distinguished. The whole combination is echoed in the sky and reflected dramatically in the canal, together with the burgeoning light patterns of the adjacent towers of downtown Indianapolis. Three artists and four sculptors were engaged on the project, as well as the writer Mary Caponegro of the American Academy in Rome. As Fulford says: 'Land architecture is a collaborative act.'[9]

It is appropriate to mention here the landscape architects for the canal system bordering the Memorial and wending its way through this part of the city. Sasaki Associates have since the 1980s skilfully renovated the canalside into which the Fulford and Reed intervention is integrated. Overall, this dramatic and varied waterside revitalization has transformed the centre of Indianapolis.

The city contains a number of memorials to war dead. Here sensory, physical reactions by people were invited, assisted by a continued reliance on oral tradition made manifest by recordings. The location and definition of the place-form itself is significant too, close to Military Park, a Civil War recruitment ground to the north. This war led to over 1,500 such medals alone, over four years, out of the 3,433 ever given and commemorated here. A more solid, masonry-heavy receptacle for the memories would have depressed the essential vitality of the historic site's potential to receive visitors. Fulford's own achievement here has been to activate and enhance the mnemonic landscape in its critical and much overlooked city-centre position.

As an inner-city intervention, the poetic vision of Fulford and Reed, and the artists also involved, has created in this Memorial a haven of transparency and illumination. It is a highly original event, unique perhaps in landscape design.

7 Meg Calkins, 'Power and Light', Landscape Architecture USA, July 2000, pp.58–60
  8 Ibid.
  9 Ibid.

Moylan School Playground
Hartford, Connecticut, USA, 1997

Mikyoung Kim

Moylan is a public school placed in a majority African-American community in the city of Hartford, Connecticut, but it is in many respects typical of similar institutions in Europe. A sense of belonging is critical to the early development of schoolchildren, and reciprocal to this is a parallel sense of individual, as well as community, ownership of the recreational space. Some degree of visual identity is essential within the playground – any negative or amorphous fenced-in and over-supervised area would be counter-productive, not only to the mission of the school, but also to the concept of recreation and play.

Mikyoung Kim has been involved in the design of no less than three playgrounds within the city of Hartford. She has negotiated innovative design through a maze of inevitably politicized school boards, and juggled resources within minimal budgets for facilities considered by some members less than essential in the range of educational priorities. She has become something of a specialist in the field of playground design, originally the subject of her research project at Harvard Graduate School of Design. A second school playground project followed immediately after Moylan. Sand School lies in another area of the town serving a predominantly Latin-American community. The project involved incorporating the playground with a new set of school buildings designed by Tai Soo Kim Partners, Architects. Here, Mikyoung Kim employed an adaptive model from Moylan for the playground. Later still, in 1996, she designed a third playground, for the McDonough Elementary School, although as yet the school has lacked the funding to proceed. She conceived a different spatial structure for the McDonough project, encouraging the children to climb over it, and perform on and around it. In other words, she sought to encourage them to play actively for each other's benefit as well as their own.

Of the three designs, the seminal and most established is that at the Moylan School. Its considerable success is proven by its appeal to more than one generation of students. The central spatial structure of the scheme is the so-called 'hide-and-seek' wall, which gives many opportunities for interpretative play. Kim had researched childrens' games, identifying visual aspects that could be interpreted in the form of a wall, and identifying with the idea of 'what you see', which is a vital ingredient of play. The wall is designed to offer 'peep holes', which make this possible in different ways. It also engages the students via the actual openings. The multiple sizes of 'windows' and 'doors' alter the speed of children running, crawling, jumping, crouching or merely ambling casually by.

The south side of the wall is divided with 'play columns' which actually establish a third space set between north and south, where north is 'public' and south is seemingly more 'private' for the purpose of play. The wall finally wraps around the east side of the courtyard to form the back of an amphitheatre.

Kim is careful to make good use of tree planting; in the centre of the playground a grove of 3-metre (10-feet) high trees provide an intermediate zone through which the students walk to and from the classroom precinct. The grove is defined at one end by a front entry, and at the other by a clear break in the 'hide-and-seek' wall. In this way it provides an area that allows the students to reorientate on leaving the street behind. Kim has so arranged the sequence that at the point where these trees cross the wall at the south side of the playground, they intersperse amongst the other elements, and break up the pattern of the paving.

The long, serpent-like wall is some 1.5 metres (5 feet) high at the highest point. It acts like a kind of elastic membrane, uniting all activity. At the same time it generates outside and inside spaces facing in opposite directions, one to the school, one towards the street beyond. The grove of honey locust trees and other species helps to define this two-way movement. Kim also added a major prefabricated play structure which integrates with the overall pattern visually, and offers an alternative source for play activity.

Teachers visiting from other schools frequently comment that there is no 'lawn', but Kim's answer is that this is an urban school within an existing street culture and defined community. She is a convincing advocate of the appropriateness of hard landscaping, and such is her proficiency in this speciality that the project has established a remarkable precedent. The Moylan School playground clearly underlines the importance of the inherent topology of any school site, and the extent to which the observational powers of children can be instrumental in responding to a positive, interactive play environment.

More specifically to Mikyoung Kim, her work emphasizes the degree to which a spatial element such as a wall, with which individuals can readily identify, can provide structuring lineaments within the urban grain at street level. Every paving detail is carefully worked out and trees and planting are used sparingly but most effectively. If Mikyoung Kim's philosophy about open space could be applied across cities, rather than in playgrounds alone, problems of urban hard landscaping could readily be solved.

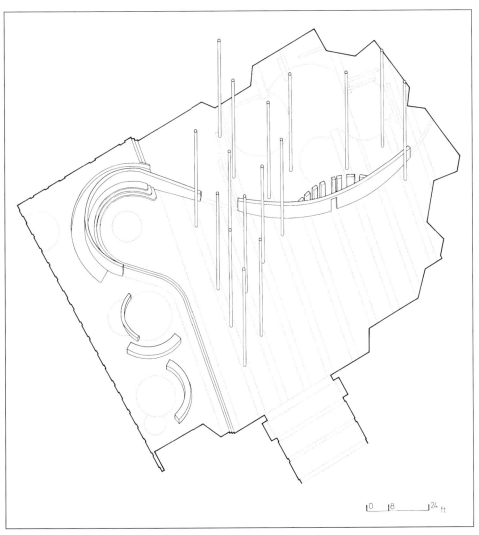

Right: Carefully grouped trees amidst various groups of 'play' landscaping

Below: The play walls are robustly constructed, and incorporate several openings

Right: Detail of stepped element and play wall

Below: Urban scale, but at the level of a child

**Promenade Plantée
Viaduc des Arts, Paris, France, 1988–96
Jacques Vergely/Philippe Mathieux/
Patrick Berger**

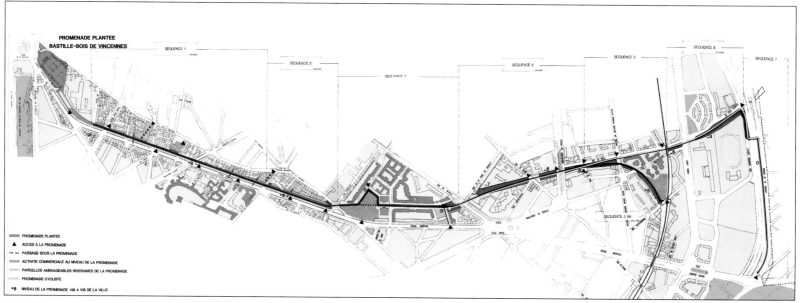

Above: Between the Place de la Bastille and the 12th arrondissement, some 4.5 km (2.7 miles) of the Promenade run along the line of the old Paris-Strasbourg railway

Opposite, above left and right: The abandoned railway becomes a green filament, animating cuttings and viaducts

Opposite, below: Intimate, carefully planned spaces are inserted along the route

An elevated promenade across the more elegant quarters of Paris would seem an unrealizable vision, desirable though it might be. It became a real possibility, however, once a proper solution had to be found for a series of abandoned railway viaducts. It suddenly became necessary for designers to animate a viaduct and two bridges, demolish a long embankment and replace it with new structures. The Promenade Plantée took a varied course, dropping down to city street level and then swooping up, twisting, winding, on routes lush with existing greenery. What was good was saved, and little of the legacy of a first machine age was ever lost. The urban *promenade architecturale* had become a landscaped artery.

The landscape designer Jacques Vergely worked closely with architects Philippe Mathieux and Patrick Berger in establishing the principles upon which new planting was to be based. This planting was the key to the design, providing new variety to contrast with mature, pre-existing vegetation. Differences in level were minimized by the creation of small squares.

Vergely had three clear objectives. Firstly, he wanted to achieve a unity of concept at the perceptual level that would be evident to the pedestrian walking by. Secondly, the site context had to be respected, especially in relation to the layered sequences of visual experience. Thirdly, the unity of the promenade as a whole was critical, despite inevitable variations in level and density of planting along the route. To this end the Crimean lime (*Tilia euchlora*), with its distinctive dark leaves with lighter undersides, was deployed in every series of alignments. Flowering cherry trees (*Prunus avium* or *Prunus padus*) were also used in groups of two to five. More

exotic species from Tibet, China and Japan were planted in isolation on the viaduct, or in the old cuttings. Such varied planting allows the season of maximum colour to be extended dramatically from autumn to the end of April. Unity of perception is further aided by the use of hornbeam in the cuttings. Box honeysuckle, with its golden and variegated foliage, was selected as well, for its seemingly indigenous appearance.

Turning now to the site context, existing vegetation in the cuttings has been developed by planting thin clearings with clumps of robinia, the robust but sinuously beautiful ailanthus (much used in London in the nineteenth century) and the ubiquitous plane tree on suitably scaled embankments. In due course these species will become high and elegant, their abundant canopies providing necessary shade in summer. Vergely also introduced some very rustic, agrarian species such as elder trees, and plants such as meadowsweet, ivy, periwinkle and forget-me-not. A degree of the wild has been fostered, robust and unexpected in this urban location, and the contrast that it creates enhances the promenade. By the use of skilled horticulture more privileged species, such as wild roses, have also been encouraged. In the spaces enclosed by hedges white rosebushes grow, and climbing roses of numerous tints.

This brilliant green filament, coursing steadily through *quartiers* so redolent of the past century, would have been inconceivable to the urban developers and architects who first rebuilt these areas, removing the dereliction of the past. It is as if the mystique, fantasy, even voyeurism of the urban park had suddenly been infiltrated in a manner that would have been quite incomprehensible to Baron Haussmann,

Right: View of the Promenade Plantée at tree level

Far right: New bridges create unbroken continuity

Opposite, above and centre left: Small, discrete spaces are interspersed with a more public articulation of planting

Opposite, below left: Long perspectives of water elements are opened up, enhancing adjoining housing

Opposite, above and below right: Urban furniture, such as stairs and seats, is carefully harmonized

Prefect of the Department of the Seine in 1853. His legacy was the largely unimpaired Paris core, still celebrated today with its culmination in the Avenue de Champs-Elysées and the Arc de Triomphe.

The railway to the Bastille was once a vital part of daily life in Paris. The removal of the locomotives from the purpose-built, elevated routes left a legacy of abandoned carriageway slicing through the twelfth *arrondissement*. The stretch of line that runs from the Place de la Bastille to the Bois de Vincennes extends for 4.5 km (2.7 miles). Originally the concession for line construction was given to the Paris-Strasbourg Company, with the right to establish the terminus at the Place de la Bastille itself. The opportunity to create a promenade on the actual viaduct became reality when the alternative scheme of demolition proved impractical. Initially, the Paris City Council, having signalled approval to the concept of a planted promenade along the line, physically made this possible by purchasing from SNCF, the state railway company which now owned the track, all the plots of abandoned line. Just prior to this, the Place de la Bastille was chosen as the site for the new Paris Opera House. By 1990, a landscape-linking promenade between Rue de Picpus and Avenue du General Michel Bizot was duly completed. In April 1990 the Reuilly mixed housing development was linked by a further stretch to the Promenade. By 1995 it was possible to travel from Avenue Ledru-Rollin to the Boulevard de la Guyane without actually leaving the Promenade.

Today, it is possible to celebrate this protracted, almost miraculous venture as something unlikely to exist anywhere else. In London it would be considered too administratively complex to maintain, in New York it would be deemed crazy not to install a light railway, and the Promenade Plantée might even be seen as a potential venue for crime, and it would be considered altogether too mundane in Vienna. In fact, it is not complicated to manage or apply proper surveillance here, possibilities for street entertainment open up, and even *le jogging* is catching on. This is Paris, after all, and the project stands as an example to less civilized cities. In 30 years' time this green filament will look as if it has always been here, since even before the age of the train. This is a unique urban event, created for the twenty-first century.

**Haas Promenade
Jerusalem, Israel, 2000
Lawrence Halprin with
Shlomo Aronson**

Above: Halprin's master concept
as landscape plan

Below: Detail of the paved way.
The olive plantations are
disturbed as little as possible

As early as 1970 Teddy Kolleck, Jerusalem's mayor at that time, formed a Jerusalem Committee to bring the city to the fore of contemporary thinking in environmental design and architecture. Such architects as Louis Kahn, Moshe Safdie and Buckminster Fuller were invited to join, and the landscape architect Lawrence Halprin, from San Francisco, was also included. A series of remarkable projects ensued, one of them being the Israel Museum. For a valley to the east of Jerusalem's centre, Lawrence Halprin himself produced a separate master-plan concept. Instrumental to this was an open space plan, with promenades designed to run along the most prominent ridge, which would prevent too much commercial development on the valley immediately below. The Tayelet, as it is called, became a defining feature in the city grain, a fortification against encroachment.

Halprin's design was produced under a clear set of guiding parameters. Views over significant features below had to decide the directional focus of the structure, and yet it would give preference to agricultural interests on the lower, fertile areas. The design character of the promenade would harmonize with these variations. Halprin was also very aware that symbolism is widely understood in Jerusalem, and so he decided to emphasize meaning in his design wherever possible. His symbolic sources were essentially ecumenical. Arches on the initial phase of the promenade were based on Christian architecture; olive groves were deliberately introduced to invoke underlying Jewish pastoralism; and Halprin made explicit an existing ley line in the amphitheatre which runs between the Islamic Mosque Al-Aksa and the Dome of the Rock, recognizing its inherent importance for the Arabic community. This multivalent symbolism was rendered benign through the philosophy of landscape design, becoming a means of linking routes and features as naturally as possible.

The first stage in the sequence was the Haas Promenade (named for the American donor). It was designed by Halprin with Shlomo Aronson as local associate. They inserted along the walkway a café and a small plaza which forms a kind of esplanade, revealing on the one hand Al-Aksa's spire and the Dome of the Rock, and on the other the historic site of the Mount of Olives, now adjacent to the Hebrew University. Both landscape architects were anxious to present the reality of the Biblical landscape before it was lost to development. And so, even the limestone of the retaining wall behind the promenade becomes rougher in texture with each course of the ascent. Thus, the landscape of olive trees and Bedouins could be saved for posterity.

The second stage of the promenade (known as the Sherover Promenade) makes the actual descent to reach the monastery below, and ultimately a plaza and restaurant. The gradient meant that flights of steps were appropriate, continuing the same idiom in detailing as before, gradually widening and opening out with descent. Here Aronson protected and emphasized the agriculture of olive groves and intervening wheat crops in winter.

Another, secondary promenade-related environment then ensues. It is called the Trotner Promenade Park. Here Aronson concentrated resources on maintaining a primarily agrarian aspect in sharp contrast to the now predominant views of the Old City beyond the valley. This section has been organized very much as a landscape park, with a more rural, meandering connotation to attract city dwellers who can then, inside the city boundaries, still experience an essentially rural environment. This is evident in the way that Aronson has used rock and flat stone with dirt paths rather than sophisticated pavings.

Yet another promenade, the Goldman Promenade, is now currently under way, sponsored by and named after a further American donor. This leads from the eastern end of the initial Haas Promenade, designed over twenty years ago, and is again an agrarian section, this time running around the hill summit eastwards again. An existing stand of mature trees is preserved amid the olive groves and grazing slopes, and as this corner wraps around the summit, the promenade reveals the undoubtedly climacteric 180-degree view of the entire valley. There is a smaller outdoor café looking out east towards the Judean heights.

What has been most significant here has been the protracted yet realistic time scale, following the initial encouragement and the establishment of the Jerusalem Committee with such vision and foresight thirty years ago. The continuity which was so vital has been maintained. Lawrence Halprin himself could draw on a long memory of the city. He was born in Brooklyn in 1916, and first visited Jerusalem in his teens, helping to found a kibbutz near to Haifa. The experience drew him back repeatedly. He was fortunate to work with Shlomo Aronson from the mid-1980s, the latter subsequently setting up his own landscape practice in Israel. The combination of skills, with Aronson in Israel, ensured a measure of control over developments – by Halprin and Aronson, then by Aronson, and finally with Halprin again – so that every stage was compatible with its predecessor. All this has happened against the varying uncertainties of politics, yet it has succeeded in establishing

Left: View down from olive groves to parkland

Right: Careful emphasis is given to the gentle landscape contours, crossed by the sinuous paved ways

its symbolism for all communities as an environment of peace and harmony, an island in a sea of turbulence. Looking at the quality of the detailing, of the various grades of masonry retaining walls, pavings and field stones, as well as the few incorporated buildings, together with the exemplary designs of the lighting stands, one becomes aware of a commitment to perfection, a recognition of natural patination and plant growth, and a wholly coherent landscape philosophy. Here is landscape that recognizes the imperatives of local views and leisure needs within a city, as well as adjusting to the symbolic needs and identification of the different ethnic groups of ancient standing in the community. Landscape design is exercised as a benignly unifying instrument where this is most needed. The fact that this remarkable combination of features and meanings, of places for activity and for reflection, exists within one of the world's most strife-torn cities can only serve to emphasize the potential of landscape design.

Above left: Conceptual sketch, establishing relationship between walls and amphitheatre

Above right: Open landscape views away from the city, with planted and conserved tree varieties

Centre left: Within the grove, stone boundaries can be used for sitting in the shade

Centre right: View towards the city

Below left: Typical edge wall, common in Jersusalem, with carefully graduated descent

Below right: Essential buildings are partly sunken to minimize landscape disruption

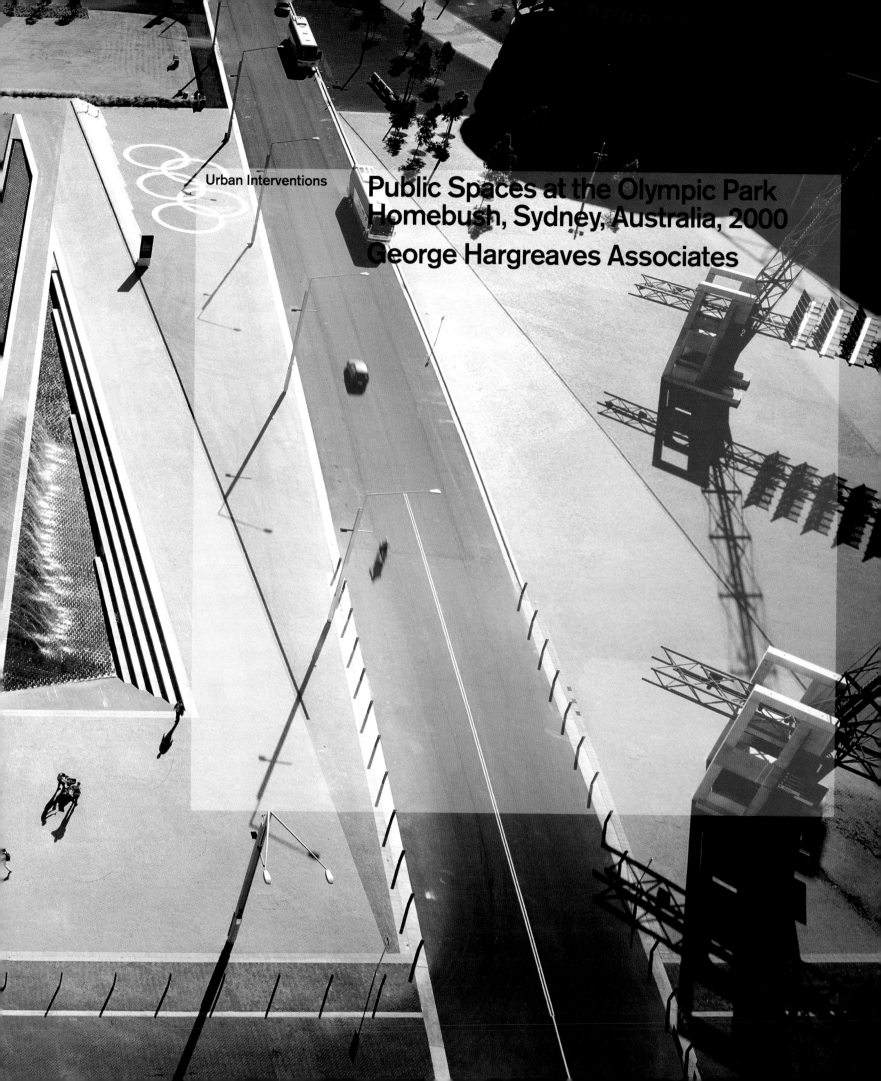

Public Spaces at the Olympic Park
Homebush, Sydney, Australia, 2000
George Hargreaves Associates

The World's best ever Olympic Games were mounted by Australia in 2000. The dramatic, final extravaganza of the Closing Ceremony, with its superb light spectacle, fireworks and the unbelievable gymnastics of the principal performers, certainly underlined the success of a uniquely well structured and organized event. In this general climate of supremacy, the unbeatable quality of the architecture and landscaping has tended to be overlooked.

The planning of hard and soft landscaping between the major stadiums and events locations began four years before the Games. Although the Homebush site lay outside the city, the overall context of scale and visitor density fell unquestionably into an urban design category, with core buildings on a city-centre scale. The spaces between the buildings were equally large. The Olympic Plaza itself became Australia's largest meeting-place, measuring 9.5 hectares (23.5 acres), and able to accommodate crowds of three million. Given that the essential structures were already planned, Hargreaves found themselves working within a pre-defined context to create urban landscape interventions on an equally massive scale.

On 14 March 1997, the first master concept design commissioned by the Olympic Co-ordination Authority from Hargreaves Associates of San Francisco was presented, in collaboration with the New South Wales Government Architect Design Directorate. The Authority had realized from the outset that the landscape had to be given the same importance as the dominant buildings on the site. The concept was articulated in terms of three 'Moves': 'Red', 'Green' and 'Blue'.

'Red' sought to define a new public domain, a single central, open place with room to accommodate massive crowds in a template of consistent paving and street furniture, with clear lighting priorities. An initial master plan draft for 'Olympic Place' was dropped, since it had lost relevance against the size of the major built enclosures.

'Green' allowed a central urban core to be established within the Millennium Park, defined by green fingers running across the Homebush Bay site from east to west, penetrating the urban core at strategic points with a diversified hierarchy of movement systems.

'Blue' incorporated water as an ordering mechanism. Fountains were located in key positions at either end of the site, at the high point of a Boulevard and at the southern edge of the Olympic Plaza that replaced the original Olympic Place. These water features were themselves part of the site water purification system, consistent with the idea of a 'green' Games.

The general resolution of scale relationships was clearly of primary importance to Hargreaves. Major object buildings proliferated on sites already set when the landscape architects began work. An inherited idea for a tree-lined boulevard proved unworkable, and trees were relocated to the periphery of the central unifying space. An 'urban forest' of dark-bark eucalypts was set in bitumen paving on a loose gridwork. The trees were planted at variable densities as it was assumed that some would be lost, and so this would not be a problem. The central space was not a passive concept, but deliberately set to 'engage' the monolithic buildings, accommodating these as interventions along its edge. It has to be remembered that the plaza was up to 170 metres (185 yards) wide, a scale similar to that of Unter den Linden in Berlin, massive by conventional urban standards. The paving pattern became instrumental along the plaza, responding to two angles, one the pre-existing grid of paddocks, buildings and service roads associated with an abattoir that once occupied the site, the other the central spine of the boulevard. The combination formed a dynamic 'way'.

A range of urban furniture, designed by the Sydney architects Tonkin Zulaikha Greer was inserted into the plaza. The most striking is a series of multi-coloured pylons. These acted as points of reference, as well as providing locations for service connections, notation, banners, phone-points, toilets, kiosks and intermediate seating. The pylons were a kind of substitute for trees, more suited in scale and context to the massive enclosures and stadiums, and interacting with the pavings to create an essentially urban piazza. The five green fingers then provided a more intimate series of transitional corridors, each running more or less at a right-angle to the plaza.

Each of the green fingers was designed with a different species of planting. The first, and northernmost, was designed with rows of *Eucalyptus citriodora* at 5-m (16-ft) intervals. The second was planted with Crows Ash (*Flindersia australis*) and Illawarra Flame Tree. The third has a wide grove of Jacaranda (*J. mimosifolia*) and Manchurian pear, providing a dense windbreak and a protracted period of flowering. The fourth green finger was designated as a 'parkway' finger, following the line of Avenue 1 at right angles to Olympic Boulevard. The fifth and southernmost finger was intended to be a more informal wetland finger, following the creek. Wetland trees are densely planted, creating more depth and perspective to be read by visitors. The wetland intersects the southern boulevard terminus at the southern plaza fountain.

The major central open space opens into two distinct halves: the paved, open plaza on the west, which joins the stadium and multi-use arena, and conversely a very lush, soft green park on the east, contrasting with the essentially hard landscaping of the plaza. Two existing features of the Homebush site are maximized in the landscape design. The first uses the existing alleys of mature indigenous eucalypts, brush boxes and figs. The second builds on and enhances the existing topography. Throughout, trees of numerous species are deployed as a mediating force in structuring an amenable, environmentally friendly scale. The trees enable

Above and below: The mangrove creek and man-made wetlands combine to form an ecological remit for the site over and above the requirement to accommodate the Olympics

Opposite, above: The Fig Grove Fountain consists of water jets arcing over pathways along a 25-m (27-yard) run

changes of scale to be established without rupturing the sequence of pedestrianized harmony. In certain areas a deliberately small-scale milieu results, mitigating the mass of the major buildings along the Plaza. Stands of trees offer shade, sanctuary and intimacy of scale where artificial structures would deny this equilibrium. Considerable attention was given to the reduction of wind effects caused both by the natural exposure of the site, and by the funnelling and turbulence effects of the taller buildings.

Key water features are used to emphasize the gradient of the site, at both high and low points. The higher event features Fig Grove Fountain, where 3-metre (10-foot) water jets arc across pathways along a 25-metre (27-yard) run. They seem to strobe in the strong sunlight, even pulsate (as in some athletic metaphor) along the grove. Ten mature figs have been retained in order to remind visitors of the historic city abattoir on this site, which the trees formerly overlooked. The water has been automatically treated, spilling into large ponds which treat waste water while aesthetically enhancing the route. The water regime is directed towards a logical recycling process throughout the site.

At the lower, northernmost point of the plaza, the existing mangrove creek (Haslams Creek) is incorporated within a 2-hectare (5-acre) man-made wetland. At this point the arcs of water rise to 10 m (32 ft), fanning downwards across granite terraces, so featuring an essential cleansing system as an aesthetic high point. The necessary 'showering' role for Californians in everyday life here meets the Australian habit on equal ground. The emblematic shower of cascades is a metaphor for the literal hygiene and cleansing process, with an ecological agenda which characterizes the entire project. The wetland ponds are replete with native plants which filter and clean storm- and surface-water as it percolates through the wetland. Finally, the water can be used for on-site irrigation or allowed to fall away into the adjacent creek and river system.

Hargreaves Associates have produced a masterly solution to a relatively new category of environmental design for the Olympic Games. They have succeeded because they recognized the fundamental dilemmas of scale confronting the organizers. The principal buildings had been already parcelled out, and sports' specifications had established beyond debate the vast scale of the key stadiums and their apparently awkward, even random, juxtapositions. The scale was definitively urban, bringing to mind the great spaces of history, of Greece and Rome, or the Forbidden City, Beijing. Without an intelligent understanding of landscape history, such scale effects would have remained discordant. Hargreaves have used the traditional urban ingredients of trees and water, of paving and street *arredamento*, but on a scale seldom experienced in urban design. The ecological agenda, so highly focused in Australia, has underpinned their ingenuity and of this, too, they have made a great success. Homebush has become a model for the articulation at urban scale of hard and soft landscape intervention. In this they have drawn upon their design for Expo '98 at Lisbon, Portugal, as well as that for Crissey Field, San Francisco, within sight of the Golden Gate bridge. Both were extremely large-scale projects, and each involved a recycling strategy. But only at Homebush was it possible for Hargreaves fully to demonstrate and resolve critical priorities in contemporary landscape design, and to bring them so successfully to fruition.

Urban Interventions

Gateshead Millennium Bridge
Gateshead, UK, 1999

Wilkinson Eyre

Above: Wilkinson Eyre's initial concept for the bridge profile

Below: The unique 'eyelid' form in plan. The bridge spans the Tyne at a slight angle

Although the River Tyne at Newcastle is famous for its bridge crossings, there has always been a void between Newcastle on the north bank and Gateshead on the south. The river itself is no great drama and, since the inevitable decline of sea freight, it has chiefly been notable for dividing the two communities at their epicentre.

Six crossings already exist over a stretch of little more than half a mile of the Tyne. The Roman Pons Aelii was built in the second century AD. This was replaced by a medieval bridge, replaced in its turn by the swing bridge built in 1876 by railway engineer George Stephenson. The double-decker, high-level bridge accommodated, for the first time in human history, rail and road travel together. The devastating result of this innovation was the separation of Henry II's medieval stronghold from its main entrance, the Black Gate, by the railway. There was little apparent regret for the destruction of the building from which Newcastle took its name. Division, perhaps, rather than unity, has long been Newcastle's forte.

Architects Wilkinson Eyre approached this riven history with some care. They realized that the bridge had to be more than an engineering solution with frills, and that a whole new concept must be evolved as a visible expression of the poetry of the river, the crossing and the joining of the two communities. The elegant new pedestrian bridge fulfils a number of practical needs, carefully elucidated by the clients. Firstly, and least evidently, it is self-cleaning. The soft-drinks cans just roll off into a bin given the right pitch. Secondly, the bridge swings upwards to allow river traffic to pass by. Next, any temptation to allow vehicles to cross has been soundly resisted. Vehicular traffic is well catered for already. It was clear that a life-enhancing pedestrian crossing would transform the two banks of the Tyne, in the same way, perhaps, as Ralph Erskine's landmark Byker Wall housing project, visible downstream of the bridge, gave new meaning to 1970s urban regeneration.

Today, it seems surprising that the Millennium Bridge, as it is called, took so long to be conceived. In 1964, just to the south in the cathedral city of Durham, the great Danish engineer Ove Arup had delivered his favourite project of all time, the Kingsgate Pedestrian Bridge across the River Wear. Kingsgate was 'state of the art' then, and the Millennium Bridge in Gateshead is today's equivalent of that important project.[10]

The immediate effect of the bridge has been to connect the new Baltic Arts Centre on the south bank with the thriving centre of Newcastle itself. This occurs in much the same way as Foster's Millennium Bridge over the Thames now links Tate Modern to the precincts of St Paul's Cathedral in the City of London. Both former industrial buildings, London's Tate Modern and Gateshead's Baltic Arts Centre, demonstrate the continual magic of the bridge as an urban catalyst. The Gateshead MBC Arts Committee has single-mindedly led the initiative through over a decade of negotiation. In terms of urban regeneration, Gateshead Council wished to link the newly regenerated Newcastle Quayside with new plans for the redevelopment of their own East Gateshead area. The bridge spans newly-created islands, running parallel to the quay-sides. Being able to access these caissons has added to the functions of the bridge, permitting a glazed hall on each one in order to provide amenities in original form, and offering outstanding new views, including that of the array of existing bridges. The new bridge running between these caissons has two parallel decks, separated by level and intermittent screening in order to differentiate between pedestrian and cycle paths. Pedestrians gain clear views over the lower cycle deck, and seating and other amenities add to the attraction of the bridge as a place with a dramatic 'place-form'.

When the bridge opens to allow shipping to pass underneath, it offers a great spectacle, the innovative rotational movement seeming akin to an eyelid slowly opening. The principle of two arches paired, one forming the deck and the other supporting this, each pivoting around a mutual point, is simple but unique in bridge design. The whole bridge in fact tilts, forming a kind of 'grand arch' and enhancing the waterside approach to both cities. This new addition has proved to be an urban intervention of a most dramatic form. The creation of a fully connected cultural node at Gateshead was utterly dependent for its success on the establishment of the bridge link. The match of the two areas has proved serendipitous, and has major implications for other waterfront or river cities.

10 Dr Francis Walley, *The Life of Ove Arup*, British Cement Association, 1995

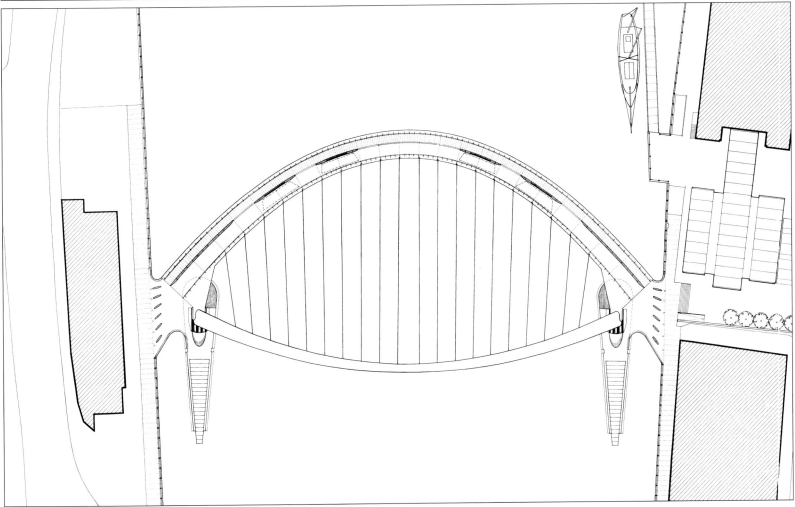

Left: Views of the Millennium Bridge during construction looking west, with the centre of Newcastle to the right. The bridge is in the closed 'eyelid' position

Below: The same view, showing the bridge rotated to allow vessels through, with the 'eyelid' open

Opposite, left: The bridge landing on the Gateshead bank

Opposite, right: Pedestrians crossing via the double way

Opposite, below: The new Baltic Arts Centre on the south bank of the Tyne

Adams, William Howard, *Roberto Burle Marx: The Unnatural Art of the Garden*, New York: Museum of Modern Art, 1991

Adams, William Howard, *The French Garden 1500–1800*, New York: George Braziller, 1979

Amidon, Jane, *Radical Landscapes: Reinventing Outdoor Space* (Foreword by Kathryn Gustafson), London: Thames & Hudson, 2001

Ardrey, Robert, *The Territorial Imperative: A Personal Enquiry into the Animal Origins of Property and Nations*, London: Collins, 1967

Argan, J C and Norberg-Schulz, C (eds.), *Roma Interrotta*, Rome: Incontri Internazionale d'Arte and Officina Edizioni, 1979

Baker, D W A, *The Civilised Surveyor: Thomas Mitchell and the Australian Aborigines*, Melbourne: Melbourne University Press, 1997

Banham, C Reyner, *Scenes in America Deserta*, London: Thames & Hudson, 1982

Bardi, P M, *The Tropical Gardens of Burle Marx*, London: Architectural Press, 1964

Barrett, J, with Bertholm, P and Marie, X, *Terrasses Jardins, Conception et Amenagement des Jardins sur Toitures, Dalles, et Terrasse*, Cordoba, Spain: Syros Alternatives, 1988

Birksted, Jan (ed.), *Relating Architecture to Landscape*, London and New York: Spon Press, 1999

Birmingham, A, *Landscape and Ideology: The English Rustic Tradition, 1740–1860*, London: Thames & Hudson, 1987

Bonner J T, (ed.), *On Growth and Form by the late Sir d'Arcy Thompson*, Cambridge University Press (abridged edition), 1961

Brown, Jane, *The English Garden in our Time: From Gertrude Jekyll to Geoffrey Jellicoe*, Woodbridge: Antique Collectors' Club, 1986

Brown, Jane, *The Modern Garden*, London: Thames and Hudson, 2002

Brett, Lionel, *Landscape in Distress*, London: Architectural Press, 1965

Buck, David N, *Responding to Chaos: Tradition, Technology Society and Order in Japanese Design*, London and New York: Spon Press, 2000

Church, Thomas, *Gardens are for People*, New York: Reinhold, 1955

Clifford, Derek, *A History of Garden Design*, New York: Praeger, 1966

Coates, S and Stetter, A, *Impossible Worlds, The Architecture of Perfection*, Basel, Boston and Berlin: Birkhauser, London: August Media, 2000

Colvin, Brenda, *Land and Landscape*, London: John Murray, 1948

Constant, Caroline, *The Woodland Cemetery – Towards a Spiritual Landscape, Erik Gunnar Asplund and Sigurd Lewerentz 1915–1961*, Stockholm: Byggforlaget, 1994

Corner, James, *Taking Measures across the American Landscape*, New Haven and London: Yale University Press, 1996

Corner, James and Balfour, Alan (eds.), *The Recovery of Landscape*, London: Architectural Association, 1995

Cosgrove, Denis, and Daniels, Stephen, *The Iconography of Landscape*, Cambridge: Cambridge University Press, 1988

Crowe, Sylvia, *Tomorrow's Landscape*, London: Architectural Press, 1956

Dawkins, Richard, *The Extended Phenotype*, Oxford: Oxford University Press, 1982

Enge, Torsten Olaf and Schroer, Carl Friedrich, *Garden Architecture in Europe 1450–1800*, Cologne Germany: Benedikt Taschen, 1990

Eckbo, G, *Landscapes for Living*, New York: F W Dodge, 1950

Fairbrother, Nan, *New Lives New Landscapes*, London: Architectural Press, 1970

Fairbrother, Nan, *The Nature of Landscape Design*, London: Architectural Press, 1974

Ferrara, Guido, *The Architecture of the Italian Landscape*, Padua: Marsilio Editori, 1968

Fieldhouse, Ken and Harvey, Sheila (eds.), *Landscape Design: an International Survey*, New York: Woodstock, 1992

Foster, Hal, *The Return of the Real: The Avant Garde at the End of the Century*, Cambridge, MA: MIT Press, 1996

Frampton, Kenneth, *Studies in Tectonic Culture: The Poetics of Construction in Nineteenth and Twentieth Century Architecture*, (ed. John Cava), Cambridge, MA: MIT Press, 1995

Fromonot, François, *Glenn Murcutt, Works and Projects*, London: Thames & Hudson, 1995

The Garden Book, London: Phaidon Press, 2000

Grishin, Sasha, *David Blackburn and the Visionary Landscape Tradition*, London and Nottingham: Hart Gallery, 2002

Gooding, Mel and Furlong, William, *Song of the Earth, European Artists and the Landscape*, London: Thames & Hudson, 2002

Gosling, David, *Gordon Cullen: Visions of Urban Design*, London: Academy Editions, 2002

Harvey, Sheila and Retting, Stephen, (eds.), *50 years of Landscape Design*, London: The Landscape Press, 1985

Heynen, Hilde, *Architecture and Modernity: A Critique*, Cambridge, MA and London: MIT Press, 1999

Hobbs, Robert, *Robert Smithson: a Retrospective View* (catalogue for the exhibition at the 40th Venice Biennale), Herbert F Johnson, Ithaca: Cornell University Press, 1982

Hoffmann, Donald, *Frank Lloyd Wright, Architecture and Nature*, New York: Dover Publications Inc., 1986

Hughes, Robert, *The Shock of the New*, London: BBC Publications, 1980

Hunt, John Dixon and Willis, Peter, *The Genius of the English Landscape Garden 1620–1820*, New York: Harper & Row, 1975

Hunt, John Dixon, *Gardens of the Picturesque: Studies in the History of Landscape Architecture*, Cambridge, MA: MIT Press, 1992

Hussey, Christopher, *The Picturesque*, London: Frank Cass & Co, Ltd., 1967

Imbert, Dorothée, *The Modernist Garden in France*, New Haven and London: Yale University Press, 1993

Jellicoe, Geoffrey, *The Guelph Lectures on Landscape Design*, Canada: University of Guelph, 1983

Jellicoe, Geoffrey and Jellicoe, Susan, *The Landscape of Man*, London: Thames & Hudson, 1975

Jellicoe, Geoffrey, *The Landscape of Civilisation*, Woodbridge: Garden Art Press, 1989

Joyes, Claire, *Monet at Giverny*, London: Mathews, Miller, Dunbar, 1975

Kastner, Jeffrey and Wallis, Brian, *Land and Environmental Art*, London: Phaidon Press, 1998

Keswick, Maggie, *The Chinese Garden*, New York: Rizzoli, 1978

Kleinert, Sylvia and Neale, Margo, *The Oxford Companion to Aboriginal Art and Culture*, Melbourne, Australia: Oxford University Press, 2000

Lancaster, Michael, *The New European Landscape* (second edition), Oxford: Butterworth Architecture, 1995

Laurie, Michael, *An Introduction to Landscape Architecture*, New York: Elsevier, 1976

Leach, Neil (ed.), *Rethinking Architecture: A Reader in Cultural Theory*, London and New York: Routledge, 1997

Lehrman, Jonas, *Earthly Paradise: Garden and Courtyard in Islam*, Berkeley: University of California Press, 1980

Libeskind, Daniel (with photo-essay by Hélène Binet), *Jewish Museum, Berlin*, Berlin: G + B Arts International, 1999

Lippard, Lucy R, *The Lure of the Local*, New York: The New Press, 1997

McDougall, E B and Hazlehurst, F H, (eds.), *The French Formal Garden, Dumbarton Oaks Colloquium on the History of Landscape Architecture, i*, Cambridge Mass: Harvard University Press, 1974

McHarg, Ian L, *Design with Nature*, New York: J Wiley & Sons Inc., 25th Anniversary Edition 1992 (first published 1967)

McKenzie, Janet, *Arthur Boyd, Art and Life*, London: Thames & Hudson, 2000

Monaco, James, *Alain Resnais*, London and New York: Secker & Warburg, 1978

Montero, Marta Iris, with Foreword by Martha Schwartz, *Burle Marx, The Lyrical Landscape*, London: Thames and Hudson, 2002

Moore, Charles W, Mitchell, William J and Turnbull, William Jr, *The Poetics of Gardens*, Cambridge, MA: MIT Press, 1988

Murray, Peter and Stevens, Mary Ann (eds.), *Living Bridges: The Inhabited Bridge, Past, Present and Future*, London: Royal Academy of Arts, and Munich and New York: Prestel, 1996

Nath, R, *Some Aspects of Mughal Architecture*, New Delhi: Abhinar Publications, 1976

Newton, Norman I, *Design on the Land: Development of Landscape Architecture*, Cambridge, MA: Belknap Press of Harvard University, 1973

Nichols, F D and Griswold, R E, *Thomas Jefferson, Landscape Architect*, Charlottesville, Virginia: University Press of Virginia, 1978

Nitschke, Gunter, *From Shinto to Ando*, London: Academy Editions, 1993

Pearsall, Derek and Salter, Elizabeth, *Landscapes and Seasons of the Mediaeval World*, London: Paul Elek, 1973

Petersen, Steen Estvard, *Herregarden I Kulturlandskapet*, Copenhagen: Arkitektens Forlag, 1975

Prest, John, *The Garden of Eden: The Botanic Garden and the Recreation of Paradise*, New Haven: Yale University Press, 1981

Richardson, Valerie, *New Vernacular Architecture*, London: Laurence King Publishing, 2001

Rosell, Quim, *Despues de Rehacer Paisajes Afterwards: Remaking Landscapes*, Barcelona: Editions Gustavo Gili SA, 2001

Rowe, Colin and Koetter, Fred, *Collage City*, Cambridge, MA: MIT Press, 1978

Rowe, Colin, *The Architecture of Good Intentions: Towards a Possible Retrospect*, London: Academy Editions, 1994

Rowe, Colin and Satkowski, Leon, *Italian Architecture of the l6th Century*, New York: Princeton Architectural Press, 2002

Rykwert, Joseph, *On Adam's House in Paradise*, New York: Museum of Modern Art in association with the Graham Foundation for Advanced Studies in the Fine Arts, Chicago, New York, 1972

Schaal, Hans-Dieter, *Landscape as Inspiration*, Berlin: Academy Editions, London/Ernst & Sohn, 1994

Schama, Simon, *Landscape and Memory*, London: Fontana Press, 1996

Schroder, Thies, *Changes in Scenery*, Basel, Boston and Berlin: Birkhauser, 2001

Scully, Vincent, *The Earth, the Temple and the Gods*, *Greek Sacred Architecure*, Cambridge, MA: MIT Press, 1963

Scully, Vincent, *Architecture, the Natural and the Man-Made*, New York: St Martins Press, 1991

Shepherd, J C and Jellicoe, G A, *Italian Gardens of the Renaissance*, London: Ernest Benn, 1925 (reprinted London: Academy Editions, 1996)

Shepherd, Peter, *Modern Gardens*, London: Architectural Press, 1953

Smith, Bernard, *European Vision and the South Pacific*, Oxford: Clarendon Press, 1960

Solkin, David H, *Richard Wilson: The Landscape of Reaction*, London: Tate Gallery, 1982

Solomon , Barbara Stauffacher, *Green Architecture and the Agrarian Garden*, New York: Rizzoli, 1988

Spens, Michael, *Gardens of the Mind. The Genius of Geoffrey Jellicoe*, Woodbridge: Antique Collectors' Club, 1992

Spens, Michael, *The Complete Landscapes and Gardens of Geoffrey Jellicoe*, London: Thames & Hudson, 1994

Spens, Michael, *Jellicoe at Shute*, London: Academy Editions, 1993

Spens, Michael, *Alvar Aalto, Viipuri Library (1927–1934)*, London: Academy Editions, 1994

Spens, Michael (ed.), *Landscape Transformed*, London: Academy Editions, 1996

Steenbergen, Clemens, *Architecture and Landscape: The Design Experiment of the Great European Gardens and Landscapes*, Munich: Prestel, 1996

Stroud Dorothy, London: Faber and Faber, 1975 (first published 1950)

Thacker, Christopher, *The History of Gardens*, London: Croom Helm, 1979

Treib, Marc and Herman, Ron, *A Guide to the Gardens of Kyoto*, Tokyo: Shufunotomo, 1980

Treib, Marc, (ed.), *Modern Landscape Architecture, A Critical Review*, Cambridge, MA: MIT Press, 1993

Tschumi, Bernard, *Cinegramme Folie: Le Parc de la Villette*, New York: Princeton Architectural Press, 1987

Tunnard, Christopher, *Gardens the Modern Landscape*, London: Architectural Press, 1938

Turner, J Scott, *The Extended Organism: the Physiology of Animal-built Structures*, Cambridge, MA and London: Harvard University Press, 2000

Turner, Tom, *English Garden Design: History and Styles since 1650*, Woodbridge: Antique Collectors' Club, 1986

Venturi, Robert and Scott-Brown, Denise, and Izenour, Steven, *Learning from Las Vegas*, Cambridge, MA: MIT Press, 1972

Verdi, Richard, *Nicolas Poussin 1594–l665*, London: Royal Academy of Arts, in association with Zwemmer, 1995

Villiers-Stuart, Constance M, *Gardens of the Great Mughuls*, London: A & C Black, 1913

Villiers-Stuart, Constance M, *Spanish Gardens, Their History, Types and Features*, London: Batsford, 1936

Walker, Peter and Sime, Melanie, *Invisible Gardens: The Search for Modernism in the American Landscape*, Cambridge, MA and London: MIT Press, 1994

Weilacher, Udo, *Between Landscape Architecture and Land Art*, Basel, Boston and Berlin: Birkhauser, 1999

Weilacher, Udo, with Foreword by Peter Latz and Arthur Ruegg, *Modern Landscapes of Ernst Cramer*, Basel, Boston and Berlin: Birkhauser, 2001

Wharton, Edith, *Italian Villas and their Gardens*, New York: Da Capo, 1976

Wilson, Colin St John, *Architectural Reflections*, Oxford: Butterworth, 1992

Wilson, Colin St John, *The Other Tradition of Modern Architecture: The Uncompleted Project*, London: Academy Editions, 1995

Wrede, Stuart and Adams, William Howard, (eds.), *Denatured Visions: Landscape and Culture in the Twentieth Century*, New York: Museum of Modern Art, 1976

Author's Acknowledgments

My first acknowledgement must be to Sir Geoffrey Jellicoe, with whom I had discussed the gestation of this book but who did not live to see it. Secondly, to the late Professor Colin Rowe, with whom key early ideas were shared, questioned and elaborated in formative discussions in London and latterly in Washington. My study of the work of Alvar Aalto, a genius mostly overlooked by these first two, but encouraged by Professor Sir Colin St John Wilson, led me myself to a fuller realization of the indivisibility in nature of landscape and architecture, and of the critical engagement of both professions within one field. Special thanks are also due to Dr Hugh Morris, and to Professor Elaine Rankin, for their continual encouragement under demanding circumstances. My colleagues at Dundee University are due a special debt of thanks for recognizing fully the needs of publication. To my initial editor, Vivian Constantinopoulos must go my thanks for her role in focussing the book, and to Iona Baird, her successor at Phaidon, for helping it steadily to fruition, ably assisted by Mel Watson as picture researcher and Helena Attlee as project editor.

Finally it must be said that this book would not finally have been realized without the support and commitment of my wife Dr Janet McKenzie, who encouraged my research in the United States, Europe, and Australia, over more than a decade. Our three children, Christiana, Flora and Mariota are also due major thanks: 'No man is an island', as John Donne said, and willingly they made bridges to be with me in support of the venture.

Michael Spens

Phaidon Press Limited
Regent's Wharf
All Saints Street
London N1 9PA

Phaidon Press Inc.
180 Varick Street
New York, NY 10014

www.phaidon.com

First published 2003
©2003 Phaidon Press
Limited

ISBN 0 7148 4155 2

Designed by Hamish Muir
Printed in Hong Kong